BEER LABELS
OF THE WORLD

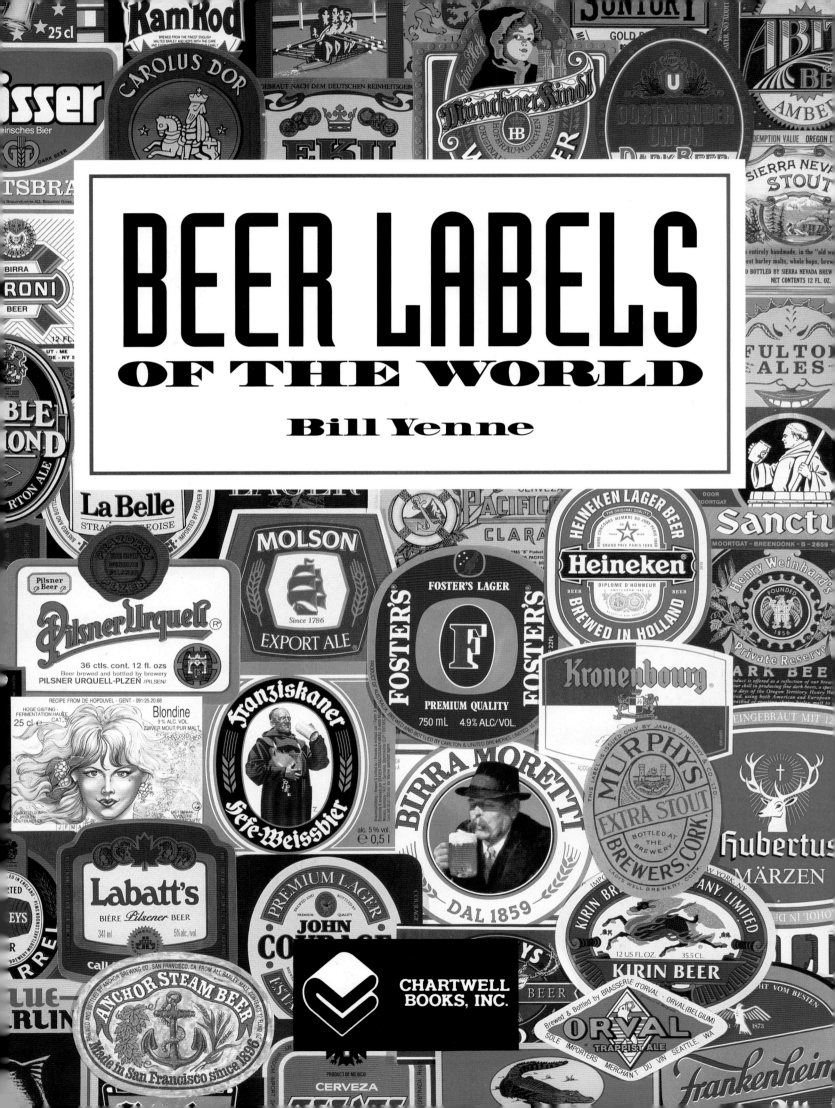

BEER LABELS
OF THE WORLD

Bill Yenne

CHARTWELL
BOOKS, INC.

Published by
CHARTWELL BOOKS, INC.
A Division of **BOOK SALES, INC.**
110 Enterprise Avenue
Secaucus, New Jersey 07094

Produced by
Brompton Books Corp.
15 Sherwood Place
Greenwich, CT 06830

ISBN 1-55521-857-1

Printed in Hong Kong

**Designed by Bill Yenne
and Tom Debolski**

Captioned by Bill Yenne

Picture credits:
Unless noted in the captions, all illustrations are reproduced by the courtesy of the brewery or brewing company depicted, except those on the following pages which are © Bill Yenne: 13, 26 (both), 33 (left), 34 (both), 47 (top), 72 (top), 73 (both), 78, 93, and 99 (top).

TABLE OF CONTENTS

INTRODUCTION

It is well known that beer was an essential part of life at the dawn of civilization, and some scholars have gone so far as to picture it as one of the very cornerstones of early civilization. Indeed, Professor Solomon Katz of the University of Pennsylvania has advanced the theory that humankind first domesticated grain not to bake bread, but to *brew beer*!

Brewing in the ancient Middle East can be dated to about 2800 BC, and often is traced back even farther. Archaeological excavations have revealed pottery containing remnants of barley and barley mash. In the early days, the art of the brewer and that of the baker were closely intertwined. Beer was brewed with barley loaves (later known as bappir), which could be eaten as bread or thrown into the brew kettle as a sort of short-cut mash. The Babylonian word for beer was *kas*, and it is seen in ancient tablets as often as the word *kasninda*, which means 'beer-loaf.' A brewer was known as a *lukasninda*, or the 'man of the beer-loaf.' Beers were also flavored with both honey and syrups prepared from dates, figs or concentrates of other fruit juices, and it was the custom of the early Babylonians, as well as the Syrians, the Hittites, the Armenians and the Greeks, to drink

their beer from large jars using straws or tubes.

Brewing and baking were equally common activities in the households of ancient Egypt. Beer was just as much of a staple as was bread, and both were routinely made in the home. The Egyptian word for brewer was *fyt*, while the process of brewing itself was known as *th*. Beer itself was known as *hkt*, *hek*, or as in Alan Eames' translation, *hekt*. This word is probably an adaptation of the old Babylonian word *hiqu*, implying a mixture, notwithstanding the Egyptian belief–recorded in an inscription on the temple at Dendera–that identifies the goddess Hathor as the 'inventress of brewing.' At Hathor's side was the goddess Menqet–the 'goddess who makes beer'–pictured in a pose reminiscent of the St Pauli Girl holding a pair of beer jars. The jackal-headed god Anubis was also pictured as being offered jars of beer.

As radical a notion as Dr Katz's theory may be, it is topped by James Death, who first wrote in 1886 that beer was 'one of the hitherto unknown leavens of Exodus.' In other words, over a century ago, Death became convinced that the Bible's *Book of Exodus (xii 15-20)* was talking about beer! He added that the admonition of Moses in *Exo-*

Above and opposite: **Beer is a wholesome beverage that has delighted and refreshed humankind for centuries.**

INTRODUCTION

Above and opposite: Beer is a wholesome beverage that has delighted and refreshed humankind for centuries.

It is well known that beer was an essential part of life at the dawn of civilization, and some scholars have gone so far as to picture it as one of the very cornerstones of early civilization. Indeed, Professor Solomon Katz of the University of Pennsylvania has advanced the theory that humankind first domesticated grain not to bake bread, but to *brew beer*!

Brewing in the ancient Middle East can be dated to about 2800 BC, and often is traced back even farther. Archaeological excavations have revealed pottery containing remnants of barley and barley mash. In the early days, the art of the brewer and that of the baker were closely intertwined. Beer was brewed with barley loaves (later known as bappir), which could be eaten as bread or thrown into the brew kettle as a sort of short-cut mash. The Babylonian word for beer was *kas*, and it is seen in ancient tablets as often as the word *kasninda*, which means 'beer-loaf.' A brewer was known as a *lukasninda*, or the 'man of the beer-loaf.' Beers were also flavored with both honey and syrups prepared from dates, figs or concentrates of other fruit juices, and it was the custom of the early Babylonians, as well as the Syrians, the Hittites, the Armenians and the Greeks, to drink their beer from large jars using straws or tubes.

Brewing and baking were equally common activities in the households of ancient Egypt. Beer was just as much of a staple as was bread, and both were routinely made in the home. The Egyptian word for brewer was *fyt*, while the process of brewing itself was known as *th*. Beer itself was known as *hkt*, *hek*, or as in Alan Eames' translation, *hekt*. This word is probably an adaptation of the old Babylonian word *hiqu*, implying a mixture, notwithstanding the Egyptian belief–recorded in an inscription on the temple at Dendera–that identifies the goddess Hathor as the 'inventress of brewing.' At Hathor's side was the goddess Menqet–the 'goddess who makes beer'–pictured in a pose reminiscent of the St Pauli Girl holding a pair of beer jars. The jackal-headed god Anubis was also pictured as being offered jars of beer.

As radical a notion as Dr Katz's theory may be, it is topped by James Death, who first wrote in 1886 that beer was 'one of the hitherto unknown leavens of Exodus.' In other words, over a century ago, Death became convinced that the Bible's *Book of Exodus (xii 15-20)* was talking about beer! He added that the admonition of Moses in *Exo-*

Above: **A delightful German bier-garten featuring the Eichbaum Bräuerei (Oaktree Brewery) whose colorful labels are also featured on its glassware.**

dus xii to abstain from leavened bread during Passover was also an admonition to abstain from beer. The fact that the consumption of wine was permitted indicates the higher level to which beer was elevated. Indeed, in the Middle Ages, the clergy–especially in the monasteries–played a vital role in preserving and developing the brewers' art.

All of this, of course, confirms that brewing and beer-drinking were common throughout the ancient world. While wine was the favored beverage of the Greco-Roman epoch, beer brewing played an important role in the daily life and culture of Northern Europe, and the traditions found today in the great brewing centers of Germany, Belgium and Britain have their roots well placed in the first millennium AD. Beer and brewing had been firmly transplanted in the western hemisphere by the eighteenth century and in Australia a century later.

Beer was originally packaged in large containers–from Mesopotamian earthenware jars to old English casks–for draft consumption, but eventually, smaller bottles in sizes below a single liter made their appearance. When bottled beer began to be mass-marketed around the middle of the nineteenth century, the bottles were usually embossed with the brewer's or bottler's name, and an added paper capsule was crimped over the cap to identify the contents and to assure the purchaser that the contents had not been tampered with.

As the range of beers increased, the embossed bottle was replaced by a plain one with a a simple label design. With the growing range of bottled beers and their increasing popularity in the early part of the twen-

A BEER IS A BEER, EXCEPT WHEN IT'S A PIVO: THE WORDS FOR BEER

Latvian: **Alus**
German, Dutch, Flemish: **Bier**
English: **Beer**
French: **Biere**
Italian: **Birra**
Spanish: **Cerveza**
Portuguese: **Cerveja**
Danish, Norwegian: **Øl**
Swedish: **Öl**
Finnish: **Olut**
Czech and Russian: **Pivo**
Polish: **Piwo**

tieth century, label designs became more colorful and imaginative.

A new art form had been created. Brewers and bottlers vied with each other to produce labels that were eye-catching as alure to potential customers. The paper capsule over the closure was replaced by a 'top strap.' Some bottles also included shoulder labels to add to the the attractiveness of the bottle, and occasionally, descriptive back labels were added as well.

With the smaller packages came the need to develop attractive labels to identify various beers, and they became common both in Europe and America toward the end of the nineteenth century as mass-merchandising of beer became more widespread. As competition within the industry increased, the labels naturally became a vital part of the marketing process.

By this time, it was common to see single-serving bottles in the now-familiar sizes—10 to 12 fluid ounces or 275 to 355 milliliters. Canned beer was first mass-marketed in 1935 as a joint development of the American

Can Company and the Gottfried Krueger Brewing Company of Newark, New Jersey. Coors introduced aluminum cans in 1959 and 'pull tabs' were first added six years later. e designs adhered to beer cans tended to mimic the paper labels used on the bottles containing the same brand of beer.

This book is intended to represent a glimpse at the state of the label-maker's art, one century after it began. Because no book of this size—or indeed *double* this size—could hope to be comprehensive, we are focusing our attention on contemporary labels, and in turn on labels which represent a range of beer styles and graphic styles. The major national brands of the world's most active brewing nations are represented, as are those of many smaller, regional brewers whose beers, or whose labels, are of particular interest to beer lovers or label collectors.

We invite you to pour yourself a glass of your favorite beer, curl up in a comfortable chair and take a tour with us through the pubs and beer cellars of the world.

–Bill Yenne

Far left: **The product line of the Feldschlosschen Bräuerei of Dresden in what used to be East Germany. The labels were introduced after German reunification in 1990.**

At left: **The familiar Fischer brand, with the boy on the label is brewed at Schiltigheim in the Alsace by Brasseries du Pecheur, France's third largest brewer.**

Top: **Putigamer of Graz is part of Austria's Steirische Group. Panther Hell is German for 'Panther Brand Pale Lager.'**

Above: **A vintage label for Whitbread's Pale Ale, traditionally one of the major products for Britain's third largest brewing company.**

READING BEER LABELS: BASIC BEER TYPES

Ale: A type of beer produced with top-fermenting yeast. It is the primary beer type in England and among North American microbreweries, but extremely rare elsewhere. It is, however, a close cousin to the German alt. Subtypes include pale ale (which is actually much more amber than pale lagers), brown ale and India pale ale, a beer developed in the nineteenth century by English brewers for export to the Empire.

Alt: The German equivalent of English or American 'ale,' literally a beer made in the 'old' way (pre-nineteenth century) with top-fermenting yeast. It is indigenous to Dusseldorf.

Barleywine: In Britain, ales with alcohol contents approaching that of wine are called barley wines.

Beer: A general term for *all* fermented malt beverages flavored with hops. The term embraces ale, lager, porter, stout and all other types discussed herein.

Bitter: A noun used in England to identify highly-hopped ale. Originally it was probably short for bitter ale. The less-used antonym is 'mild,' also a noun.

Bock: An especially strong, dark lager occasionally, but not necessarily, produced in concordance with spring festivals.

Cream ale: A blend of ale and lager invented in the early twentieth century by American brewers.

Diat: A German word for lager low in carbohydrates originally developed for diabetics. It is *not* a 'diet' or low-calorie beer.

Doppelbock: A German word literally meaning 'double bock.' Although it is not nearly twice as strong, it is typically the highest alcohol beer style brewed in Germany. In naming practice, doppelbocks are given names ending in 'ator,' such as Celebrator, Salvator or Optimator.

Dunkel (Dunkles): A German adjective used to describe a dark lager, usually in the sweeter Munich style.

Eisbock: A German term that originated in Dortmund and applied to especially flavorful and powerful light-colored lagers.

Faro: A light, sweet Belgian lambic favored in Brussels.

Framboise/Frambozen: A Belgian lambic flavored with raspberries.

Gueuze: Blended Belgian lambic beers not containing fruits.

Hell (Helles): An adjective used to describe lager that is pale in color.

Keller: A German-style of packaged, unfiltered lager that emulates *vom fass* (on draft) beer.

Kriek: A Belgian lambic flavored with cherries. Probably the most popular of the fruit lambics.

Lager: This beer style accounts for well over 90 percent of the beer brewed and marketed in the world (outside England). Specifically, it is a clear, pale beer fermented with bottom-fermenting yeast at nearly freezing temperatures. The fermentation period is also longer than that for ale and hence the name, which is German meaning 'to store.'

Lager had its origins in the heart of central Europe in an area that the author likes to call the Golden Triangle. This triangle is so named because of the golden color of lager itself and because of the success that brewers had with this product when it was first developed for widespread commercial sale in the early to middle nineteenth century. The corners of the Triangle lie in Munich, Prague and Vienna, the capitals, respectively, of Bavaria (a state of the German republic), Bohemia (Czechoslovakia) and Austria.

Lambic: A style of beer fermented with special strains of wild yeast indigenous only to Belgium's Senne Valley. One of the world's most unique native beer styles.

Leicht: The German word for 'light,' or low-calorie beer.

Maibock: A bock beer brewed for release in May.

Malt liquor: A term imposed by the American government to identify beer with an alcohol content above five percent. It is not actually a true beer type as the term may be imposed on ales or lagers.

Some larger American brewers produce very pale high-alcohol lagers and call them malt liquors.

Moorzen: Originally this German term was used to describe a reddish lager brewed in March and set aside for summer. The style is now brewed for autumn consumption, particularly in connection with Oktoberfest.

Peche: A Belgian lambic flavored with peaches that has become increasingly popular in recent years.

Pils: A German term for pale, Pilsen-style lagers.

Pilsener or Pilsner: The most widely known and widely imitated lager type, it is named for Pilsen in Bohemia (Czechoslovakia) where it originated in the early nineteenth century. It is typically the lightest, sweetest and palest of lagers. The Plzensky Prazdroj brewery in Pilsen brews Pilsner Urquell ('Pilsner from the original source'), which is considered the definitive pilsner, although the term has become generic.

Porter: A dark, sweet beer brewed with top-fermenting (ale type) yeast that was developed in London in the late eighteenth century and revived by American microbrewers in the late twentieth century.

Rauchbier: A lager with a strange and wonderfully smoky flavor produced in and around Bamberg, Franconia in Germany, using malt that has been roasted over a very smoky beechwood fire.

Reinheitsgebot: The German purity law of 1516 which required brewers to use only malt, yeast, hops and water in making all beer sold in Germany. Since Germany's admission to the European community, the Reinheitsgebot has not been legally binding since 1987, but German brewers still proudly follow it. In the United States, microbreweries generally follow the Reinheitsgebot, but the larger breweries use numerous fillers, adjuncts and additives.

Stout: A dark, creamy beer produced with top-fermenting (ale type) yeast. Stout is the prominent beer type in Ireland and is widely available in England. Also brewed occasionally by microbreweries in the United States, it is rare elsewhere. Guinnness, brewed in Dublin and London, is the definitive stout of the Irish type. English brewers, such as Samuel Smith in Tadcaster, also produce oatmeal stout in which oats are used along with barley malt.

Weissbier: A German word literally meaning beer that is white (weiss), but actually implying a style of pale-colored, top-fermented beer made with about half wheat malt (*see facing page*). It is typical of Berlin and northern Europe. A **hefe-weiss** beer is a weissbier in which yeast sediment remains in suspension in the beer. Weiss bier is also known as **weizenbier**, but should not be confused with **wiesenbier**, which is a festival beer that may or may not contain wheat malt.

Witbier/Biere Blanche: Flemish/French literally meaning white (wit) beer. It is brewed using over half wheat malt. A cousin to German Weissbier, Witbier is indigenous to the northern, Flemish-speaking areas of Belgium.

THE UNITED KINGDOM

Above: **Bass Brewing, the largest brewer in Britain, has the world's oldest beer trademark** *(see text, at right).*

Below: **The product line of Bateman's Brewery which has been brewing in Yorkshire since 1874.**

Facing page: **A John Courage tied house in London as photographed by the author.**

In any consideration of British beer labels, the obvious place to begin is with Britain's (and arguably the *world's*) oldest registered trademark–the familiar red triangle of Bass & Company. According to General Certificate Number 1 of the Patents Designs & Trade Marks Act, it was registered on 25 July 1890, but is sworn to have been in use since before 31 December 1855, and the company itself dates to 1777. The label was also featured in the 1883 painting *The Bar at the Folies Bergeres*, painted by Edouard Manet shortly before he died.

Despite the advent of North America's new plethora of ale-brewing microbreweries in the 1980s, Britain remains the only major brewing nation in the world where ale is the dominant form of beer being consumed. Ale is defined as beer which is fermented with bottom fermenting yeast at a low room temperature. This contrasts with lager, the world's dominant beer type, which is fermented longer with bottom fermenting yeast at near-freezing temperatures. The two types of beer are typically served at roughly the same temperatures as they are fermented, so to a world used to cold lager, the British have always been considered a mite peculiar for their love of 'warm' beer.

Today as real ale is becoming more and more popular in North America and lager is enjoying an increasing market share in the United Kingdom, old distinctions are blurring, but ale is still the characteristic beer of the United Kingdom.

Bass is the largest brewer in the United Kingdom today, followed by Allied-Lyons Breweries (Ind Coope), Whitbread, Watney, John Courage and Scottish & Newcastle, with Ireland's Guinness operating a brewery in London and enjoying a sizable market share. The 'Big Six' British brewing companies control 80 percent of the market, but there is also a generous mix of both old-line small regional brewers and newly-formed microbreweries in England. The campaign for Real Ale (CAMRA), which was born in Manchester in 1972, has done a great deal to compel the big brewers to brew quality products, and to support the smaller brewer who maintain high standards.

Despite the fact that there are over 20 breweries in London, Burton-Upon-Trent is the historic center of Britain's brewing industry, due largely to the quality of the water drawn from local artesian wells. Bass was born here, as was Worthington's White Shield Brewery, with which Bass would eventually merge. The water contains gypsum and is perfect for brewing, a fact that had been observed as early as 1002 AD when the Benedictine Monastery of Saint Modwen was founded. The monks, who brewed their own ale, noted an improvement after they moved to Burton, yet the only thing that had changed was the water they had been using. The Burton Abbey brewhouse continued its daily output of beer until the early seventeenth century when it was taken over by William Paget, secretary to Henry VIII.

By 1600, Burton had 46 inns with attached brewhouses (brewpubs). A century later, commercial breweries began to appear on the shores of the River Trent, which had become a major thoroughfare for shipping traffic after passage of the Trent Navigation Act in 1669. In 1777, William Bass, who ran a

Above: **Burton brewer William Worthington was a prime competitor of William Bass in the late eighteenth century, but their firms ultimately merged.**

Below: **This Adnam's draft handle, so tastefully photographed in a Suffolk pub, features the same logo as the corresponding ESB label.**

business hauling ale to London, opened his own brewery in Burton. He died 10 years later, but his son Michael carried on the business, and by 1800, he had a thriving trade exporting beer to the Baltic countries, Russia and to Danzig and other German states. However, in 1806, Napoleon banned imports of British ale to Europe, and Bass' business, along with that of all British brewers, suffered. It was not until the end of the Napoleonic wars that business picked up again.

In 1832, recalling Napoleon's boycott and perceiving the potential of the British Empire market, Bass developed a new beer in Burton which was called 'India Pale Ale.' It was so named because it traveled well, even to distant India, as well as to Egypt and South Africa. India Pale Ale also sold well in the reopened Baltic market.

Ironically, Bass never fully exploited the market within Britain–except for London, Liverpool and Burton itself–until the opening of the railway through Burton in 1839, which eventually led to opening up the entire United Kingdom market. This contributed to the success of Bass and Burton's brewing industry in general, and a remarkable expansion took place. By the Bass centennial in 1877, output had reached a million barrels

(1.2 million hectoliters) annually, and the bottles with the little red triangle were being sold on America's Union Pacific Railroad. Meanwhile, across town, Charrington, with whom Bass would ultimately merge, was already brewing 80,000 barrels (95,000 hectoliters).

Today both Bass and Ind Coope remain as the flagships in Britain's capital of brewing. Ind Coope–now the cornerstone of Allied-Lyons and Britain's second largest brewing company–began at the Star Inn in Romford during the mid-eighteenth century when the innkeeper there started brewing beer and his reputation quickly spread. In 1779, Edward Ind purchased this thriving business and John Smith successfully managed it. In 1845, WOE Coope and his brother George bought Smith out, and the brewhouse of the Star Inn became the Romford Brewery, and the firm of Coope & Company was established. Though the Romford Brewery was successful, the company was attracted to Burton because of the water and the fact that it was clearly the center of the British brewing industry.

In 1856, Ind Coope bought a new brewery on Burton's Station Street adjoining the Allsopp Brewery. Soon Ind Coope was brewing its own Burton ales, including an India Pale Ale, which they branded with the Double Diamond symbol. Within a few years, both Ind Coope and Allsopp's became household names, and in 1934 they merged their businesses to form Ind Coope & Allsopp's, joining their premises to form what today is Ind Coope Burton Brewery. The well-known Skol brand was first brewed in 1973, and currently Ind Coope Burton Brewery exports to over 40 countries, from Russia to the West Indies.

The third largest brewing company in Britain dates back to when Samuel Whitbread the elder was born on 20 August 1720 in a village near Bedford. At the age of 16, he was apprenticed to work in a brewery in the city of London, which was owned by John Wightman, Master of the Brewers' Company. In 1742, Whitbread formed a partnership and began brewing in London's Whitecross Street.

In 1722, a strong, black beer was introduced which used coarse barley and hops that were suited for London's soft water. It mainly appealed to market porters, who liked both its body and its price. Hence, it became known as 'porter.' The real advantage of porter became clear later when it was made in bulk: it did not deteriorate if matured in wooden casks over a long period of time. No one saw the potential of porter more clearly than Whitbread. By 1750, he had built a new brewery specifically designed for its mass production. Soon porter became

Above: **Burton brewer William Worthington was a prime competitor of William Bass in the late eighteenth century, but their firms ultimately merged.**

Below: **This Adnam's draft handle, so tastefully photographed in a Suffolk pub, features the same logo as the corresponding ESB label.**

business hauling ale to London, opened his own brewery in Burton. He died 10 years later, but his son Michael carried on the business, and by 1800, he had a thriving trade exporting beer to the Baltic countries, Russia and to Danzig and other German states. However, in 1806, Napoleon banned imports of British ale to Europe, and Bass' business, along with that of all British brewers, suffered. It was not until the end of the Napoleonic wars that business picked up again.

In 1832, recalling Napoleon's boycott and perceiving the potential of the British Empire market, Bass developed a new beer in Burton which was called 'India Pale Ale.' It was so named because it traveled well, even to distant India, as well as to Egypt and South Africa. India Pale Ale also sold well in the reopened Baltic market.

Ironically, Bass never fully exploited the market within Britain—except for London, Liverpool and Burton itself—until the opening of the railway through Burton in 1839, which eventually led to opening up the entire United Kingdom market. This contributed to the success of Bass and Burton's brewing industry in general, and a remarkable expansion took place. By the Bass centennial in 1877, output had reached a million barrels

(1.2 million hectoliters) annually, and the bottles with the little red triangle were being sold on America's Union Pacific Railroad. Meanwhile, across town, Charrington, with whom Bass would ultimately merge, was already brewing 80,000 barrels (95,000 hectoliters).

Today both Bass and Ind Coope remain as the flagships in Britain's capital of brewing. Ind Coope—now the cornerstone of Allied-Lyons and Britain's second largest brewing company—began at the Star Inn in Romford during the mid-eighteenth century when the innkeeper there started brewing beer and his reputation quickly spread. In 1779, Edward Ind purchased this thriving business and John Smith successfully managed it. In 1845, WOE Coope and his brother George bought Smith out, and the brewhouse of the Star Inn became the Romford Brewery, and the firm of Coope & Company was established. Though the Romford Brewery was successful, the company was attracted to Burton because of the water and the fact that it was clearly the center of the British brewing industry.

In 1856, Ind Coope bought a new brewery on Burton's Station Street adjoining the Allsopp Brewery. Soon Ind Coope was brewing its own Burton ales, including an India Pale Ale, which they branded with the Double Diamond symbol. Within a few years, both Ind Coope and Allsopp's became household names, and in 1934 they merged their businesses to form Ind Coope & Allsopp's, joining their premises to form what today is Ind Coope Burton Brewery. The well-known Skol brand was first brewed in 1973, and currently Ind Coope Burton Brewery exports to over 40 countries, from Russia to the West Indies.

The third largest brewing company in Britain dates back to when Samuel Whitbread the elder was born on 20 August 1720 in a village near Bedford. At the age of 16, he was apprenticed to work in a brewery in the city of London, which was owned by John Wightman, Master of the Brewers' Company. In 1742, Whitbread formed a partnership and began brewing in London's Whitecross Street.

In 1722, a strong, black beer was introduced which used coarse barley and hops that were suited for London's soft water. It mainly appealed to market porters, who liked both its body and its price. Hence, it became known as 'porter.' The real advantage of porter became clear later when it was made in bulk: it did not deteriorate if matured in wooden casks over a long period of time. No one saw the potential of porter more clearly than Whitbread. By 1750, he had built a new brewery specifically designed for its mass production. Soon porter became

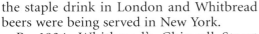

Above and below: A label and pub draft handle bearing the mark of Ind Coope.

Left: The labels for both the Morland bottles and the pub handles have coordinated designs.

the staple drink in London and Whitbread beers were being served in New York.

By 1834, Whitbread's Chiswell Street brewery had begun to brew ale, and in 1869, Francis Manning-Needham introduced the concept of bottled beer to the business. By the outbreak of the first World War, more than half of the brewery's output of nearly one million barrels (1.2 million hectoliters) a year was being bottled. Whitbread had become one of the pioneers of packaged beer, along with Worthington and Bass. Brewing finally ceased in Chiswell Street in 1976, and most of Whitbread's beer is now produced at Luton and Salmesbury.

The fourth of the Big Six is Watney, which dates its beginning to 1487 and which later merged with Combe Reid in 1898. Although the official name would thereafter be Watney Combe Reid, it is always referred to as 'Watney' or 'Watney's.' Watney's in turn merged with Mann, Crossman & Paulin in 1958, but the name remained Watney's.

In 1787, John Courage, the Scottish-born son of an exiled French Huguenot family, bought a small brewery in Southwark, London on the south bank of the Thames. Southwark brewing was already renowned, and indeed Chaucer noted its prowess in the fourteenth century *Canterbury Tales*. Shakespeare based Falstaff on one of Southwark's leading brewing figures, Pepys viewed the

Great Fire of London in 1666 from a Southwark ale house, and Dr Samuel Johnson earned a few quid as an investor in the Thrale family brewery.

Having founded what is today the fifth of Britain's Big Six, Courage developed valuable international commerce from his site on the Thames. Trade with the Royal Navy led to the spread of the Courage name throughout the English-speaking world. Interestingly, the origins of John Courage Amber Lager go back in years to a specially developed export beer that rapidly became the Navy's own brand. In fact, it eventually replaced the seaman's daily tot of rum when the Royal Navy ended that long-standing tradition. In 1896, however, the John Courage group was purchased by Elders IXL, the Australian group best known as the worldwide distributor of Foster's Lager.

Rounding out the Big Six is Scottish & Newcastle, Ltd, which was formed in 1960 by a merger of Scottish Brewers, Ltd and Newcastle Breweries, Ltd.

Among the notable smaller breweries in Britain is Samuel Smith's Old Brewery at Tadcaster. The oldest brewery in Yorkshire was founded by his family. Both Dr Samuel Johnson and Oliver Goldsmith frequented Samuel Smith's Tadcaster pubs, and Charles Dickens describes the brewery in his *Tale of Two Cities*.

At Right: Since 1641, there had been references to the fine beers of Southwold at Sole Bay. The brewery appears to have evolved from the old brewhouse behind the Swan Hotel, the most important inn in Southwold. The name Adnams first appeared in 1872 when the Adnams family arrived from Berkshire to take over the Sole Bay Brewery. A great many medals, cups and awards have been won over the years, pride of place going to the Championship Cup for the Best Beer in Britain, awarded for Champion Pale Ale at the National Brewers' Exhibition, Wine Merchant of the Year in 1991, and First Prize Standard Bitter, awarded at the Great British Beer Festival in 1990.

At right: Bateman's Brewery was founded in Lincolnshire in 1874 and is still family owned and operated. The current beers have won many awards, including the Campaign for Real Ale (CAMRA) Beer of the Year.

Also at right: John Courage began brewing in 1787, founding what is today, the fifth largest British brewing Company.

At right: The Felinfoel *(fay-lin-voyl)* Brewery is located near the city of Swansea in Wales. Established in 1878, it has been in the family of the founder ever since.

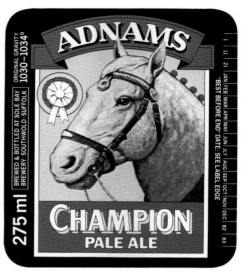

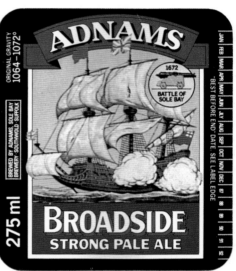

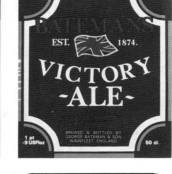

At right: Founded in 1845, Fuller's is one of the capital city's chief local brewers. Extra Special Bitter (ESB) is a classic ale.

At right: The Gibbs family have been brewers since the eighteenth century. Gibbs Mew was formed in 1898 to take over the businesses of Bridger Gibbs & Sons and Herbert Mew & Co, both of Salisbury. The company still uses the exclusive water from its own well. Gibbs Mew boasts a string of prizes for its brews, such as the Brewing Industry's Gold Medal for its Moonraker Brown Ale.

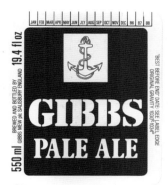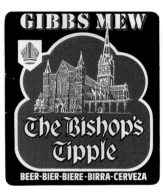

At right: Charles Hall founded the Ansty Brewery in 1777. With England at war against France, a large military encampment was set up at Weymouth to counter the threat of invasion. The young brewer quickly secured a government contract for the supply of Ansty Beer to the camp. After the purchase of other local breweries and their houses at the turn of the century, Ansty became a Limited Company and moved into a new brewery at Blandford St Mary, the company's present headquarters, built at a cost of 28,000 pounds. The brothers George Edward and Alfred Woodhouse were the two directors, joined by their youngest brother Frank, who died while serving as chairman in 1952. Since Charles Hall founded the brewery, Hall & Woodhouse has won many National brewing awards for their excellent beers. Badger Best Bitter, a traditional beer dispensed mostly by hand pumps, is now available at brew houses in Devon, Hampshire, Berkshire, Surrey, Middlesex, Sussex and Avon, in addition to the Badger area of Dorset, Somerset and Wiltshire.

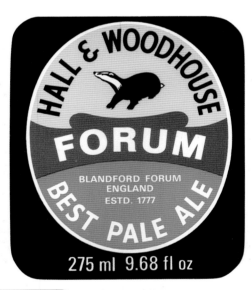

At right: Thomas Hardy's Ale from Dorchester is a strong ale that is highly sought by connoisseurs for its extraordinary flavor.

At right: Allied-Lyons dates back to the Ind Coope partnership of the early nineteenth century. The Allsopp name was one of Burton's most prominent brands, both before and after it's becoming part of the Ind Coope Empire. Double Diamond is the flagship Ind Coope beer and the Skol brand was introduced in 1973.

Also at right: Allied-Lyons also produces the regional brands Friary Meux, Tetley and Harry Ramsden's Yorkshire Ale.

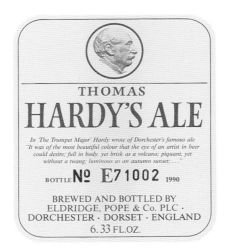

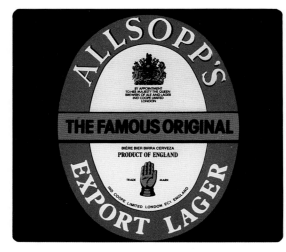

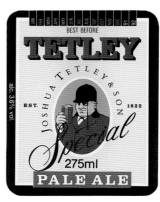

At right: Established in 1711, Morland is England's second oldest independent brewer, with over 200 pubs, mostly in the Thames Valley region. The Morland 'sign of the artist' dates back to the eighteenth century when George Morland, a relative of the brewing Morlands and one of the region's more well-known painters of that era, was a frequent guest at Morland hostelries. It was in tribute to him that the family chose the artist as their symbol. Pallet in one hand, pint in the other, the Morland logo honors both the painter's and the brewer's art.

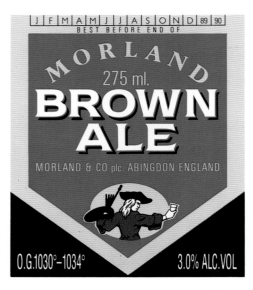

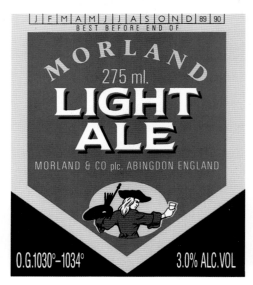

At right: The beers of Samuel Smith's Old Brewery in Tadcaster include the extraordinary Taddy Porter, Nut Brown Ale, Imperial Stout (reminiscent of the beers brewed in England during the eighteenth century for the Baltic market) and Oatmeal Stout. The labels were designed by Charles Finkel of Merchant du Vin, the company that imports the line into the United States.

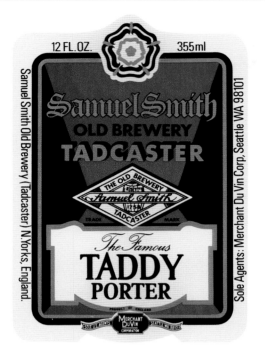

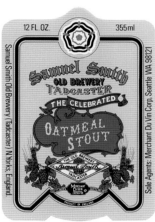

At right: Scottish & Newscastle was formed by the 1960 cross-border merger of Scottish Brewers, Ltd and Newcastle Breweries, Ltd. The popular flagship brands of the two components are still seen in the labels, however.

At right: As the Napoleonic Wars reached their end, Tennents began to expand its markets into England, and beer was shipped form the Clyde Coast to Liverpool and Bristol. Hugh Tennent, the son of this well-established Glasgow brewing family, introduced lager into Scotland in 1885. He had discovered the light colored beer in Europe and suggested that the family company should begin producing it in Scotland. Today lager is the most popular Scottish beer and Tennent's Lager has been Scotland's top-selling lager since it first appeared.

At right: Vaux & Sons was founded in 1837 by Cuthbert Vaux at a brewery in Sunderland. In 1927, Vaux & Sons, Ltd merged with North Eastern Breweries, Ltd, Associated Breweries. Lorimer & Clark, Ltd's Caledonian Brewery in Edinburgh, Scotland, is a Vaux subsidiary.

At right: Watney Combe Reid & Company, whose brewing heritage dates to 1487, operates breweries in London and Isleworth, Middlesex. Watney's Red Barrel is one of Britain's best-known beers. Brewed by Watney's, Cream Stout is based on a seventeenth century recipe.

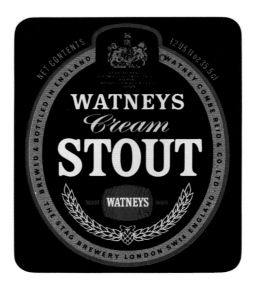

At right: In 1876, Charles Wells retired retired from the sea, and bought a small brewery at Horne Lane in Bedford. His sons continued to develop the business by taking over other brewing companies in and around Bedford, by acquiring more public houses, and by continuing the policy of developing existing pubs. A new brewery at the edge of Bedford was completed in 1976.

At right: The product line of Whitbread, Britain's third largest brewing company.

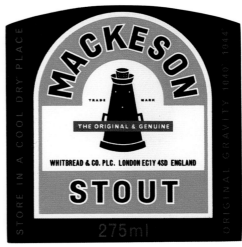

At right: Young & Company's Ram Brewery evolved from a brewery that existed on the River Wandle at Wandsworth (London) in 1675. Charles Allen Young bought the Ram Brewery in 1831. Today Young's–still a Young family business–owns over 150 tied houses, mostly in and around London, and brews a variety of beers for bottling. These have won numerous awards, both from the industry and from the Campaign for Real Ale (CAMRA).

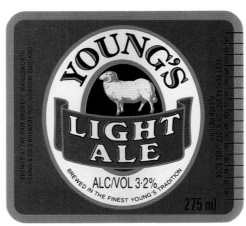

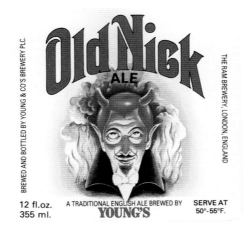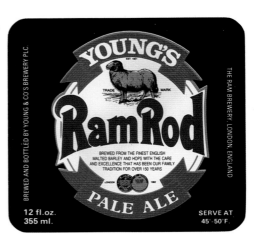

IRELAND

In a world of lager breweries, where the United Kingdom is the only major brewing nation whose primary beer style is ale, Ireland is the only nation where the primary beer style is stout. Like ale, stout is produced with top-fermenting yeast. However, it derives its nearly black color from the barley and barley malt used in the brewing process, which is roasted until it is a very dark brown.

The major brewer of stout in Ireland, and indeed in the world, is Arthur Guinness & Sons of Dublin. The other major Irish brewing companies—Murphy and Beamish—are located in Cork, the Republic of Ireland's second largest city.

By the end of the twelfth century, a considerable amount of ale was brewed in Dublin along the course of the Poddle River, whose water was considered ideal for the purpose. Writing in 1610, Barnaby Rych in his *New Description of Ireland* gave an account of the brewing industry in Dublin during that period. At that time, it was estimated that there were 1180 ale houses and 91 brew pubs in the city of Dublin, whose population was approximately 4000 families. During the eighteenth century, the brewing of beer passed gradually from the hands of small pub brewers and home brewers to those of commercial brewers, who had been incorporated in Dublin by Royal Charter in 1696.

St James' Gate, which has given its name to the Guinness brewery, was the ancient entrance to the outer city from the suburbs of Dublin. It is shown on Speed's map of Dublin (1610) and on Brooking's map of Dublin (1728), and it stood close to where the main gate of the Guinness Brewery is now situated. The area of the city of Dublin adjacent to St James' Gate had, from very early times, been a favorite neighborhood for breweries, because it lay on the main road to the capital from the grain-growing districts of central Ireland. The main supply of water to the city, derived from the Poddle River, passed through the area before entering the city proper. On 31 December 1759, Arthur Guinness of County Kildare came here and took over a brewhouse on a lease of 9000 years 'to be held in as ample and as beneficial a manner as the same was formerly held.'

At that time the duty on beer imported from England was merely a fraction of a shilling per barrel, while that brewed in Ireland was taxed at 5 shillings per barrel. Ireland could hardly hope to compete with imported beer under such circumstances.

Below: **The Beamish & Crawford line of packaged products surround a pub draft handle.**

Above and left: Familiar icons: The label of Dublin's Guinness and a pub sign of Murphy's in Cork city.

Nevertheless, Arthur Guinness struggled on and became successful. It didn't hurt that in 1782, the legislative independence of Ireland was established by the British parliament.

Henry Gratton, who later supported the Dublin brewers before the Irish Parliament, wrote to Arthur Guinness that he regarded St James' Gate Brewery as 'the actual nurse of the people, entitled to every encouragement.'

From that date, Guinness went on to capture the Irish and London markets–and eventually the markets of the world. During the early decades of the twentieth century, the St James' Gate Brewery in Dublin was the largest brewery in the world, and, although it has since been surpassed, it is still one of the world's major brewing centers.

James J Murphy and Company, Ltd was founded in 1856 at Lady's Well in Cork by the the four Murphy brothers, James, William, Jerome and Francis. The Lady's Well name derived from a celebrated well on the hill opposite the premises which was dedicated to the Virgin Mary and believed to possess miraculous properties. To the present day,

pilgrims make their way to the shrine each year in May. In the eighteenth century, Cork was considered to be an excellent location for a brewery. There the finest of malting barley from the country's limestone soils was combined with the pure water of the city to produce the creamy, mellow flavor of Murphy's Irish Stout.

In the nineteenth century, Lady's Well was one of Cork's largest breweries. Initially, Murphy's Brewery brewed porter but switched to stout, which it has brewed ever since. In 1975, James J Murphy signed a licensing agreement with the Netherlands' largest brewing company to brew Heineken for the Irish market, and a marketing company, called Heineken Ireland, Ltd, was set up. In 1983, the Murphy Brewery was purchased by Heineken International, which immediately initiated a huge investment by building a new brewery on the same site as the old plant. Murphy's was relaunched with a new label, and is now exported and promoted at home and abroad using Heineken's international marketing clout.

At right: The Guinness product line includes both the world famous Stout (with both domestic and export labels seen here), Harp Lager and Kaliber nonalcoholic lager.

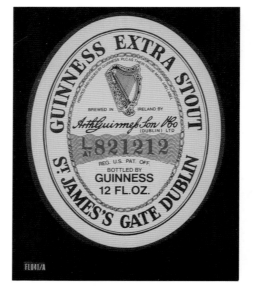 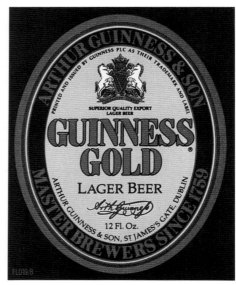

At right: An evolution of Beamish & Crawford label designs.

At right: Label designs from the James J Murphy & Company's Lady's Well Brewery in County Cork.

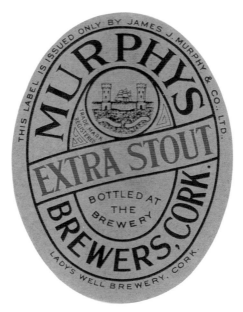 

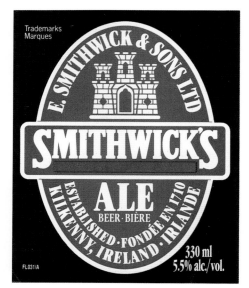

At right: Formerly independent breweries now owned by Guiness: In addition to its flagship plant at St James' Gate and a plant in England, Arthur Guinness & Sons also owns Cherry's Breweries at Waterford, McCardle Moore in Dundalk and E Smithwick & Sons in Kilkenny (*top row right*).

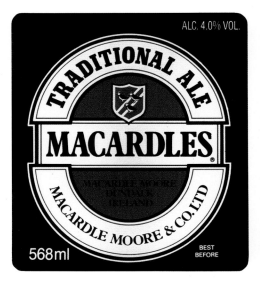

THE NETHERLANDS

Above: **A street scene in rainy Amsterdam with both Heineken and Amstel signs prominently displayed.**

Below: **Heineken's flagship brewery in Amsterdam is now a showplace, having been eclipsed by the company's larger breweries elsewhere.**

There is the story of the man who went to the Netherlands and was confused because all the streets seemed to have the same name. He explained that there was a neat red and white sign on every street corner in every city, every town and every village, but that they all said the same thing: Heineken.

It may not be true that there are more Heineken signs than street signs in the Netherlands, but certainly no brand dominates its country of origin as completely as the flagship brand of Heineken NV. Indeed, the labels of this Amsterdam-based brewing company are ubiquitous, not only in its home country, but around the world. There is probably no brand with the global market penetration of Heineken, and the company is in fact the largest brewer on earth, after the two American giants Anheuser-Busch and Miller.

The story of Heineken began in 1863 when Gerard Adriaan Heineken told his mother of his ambitious business proposal that he thought could be the answer to her prayers to rid Amsterdam's Sunday-morning streets of wayward souls who had enjoyed too much of their homemade brews the night before. Gerard proposed that the only way to get people to stop drinking hard liquor was to offer a lighter alternative–of a consistent quality. If she would only provide the money, he could do just that. Heineken had his eye

on an old brewery, *De Hooiberg,* The Haystack, a well-known Amsterdam establishment dating from 1592. After convincing his mother of the merits of his plan, he bought the building in 1864 and began brewing lager. Soon afterward, he built another brewery just outside the city limits, and in 1874 he expanded even further, with the opening of a brewery in Rotterdam.

Whether or not Heineken succeeded in ridding Amsterdam of its drunks is not known, but he quickly became one of his nation's most successful brewers. With a domestic market share and production base firmly in place, the way was paved for exports to France and other European markets. By the turn of the century, Heineken beer was on its way to markets in the Far East.

On 14 April 1933, soon after the repeal of Prohibition, Heineken became the first European beer imported into the United States. Today Heineken remains the number one imported beer in the United States and throughout the world. Heineken's distinctive green and white cartons have actually become the largest single commodity shipped in bulk from Europe to America each year. In fact, the Heineken company proudly notes that it has exported more beer than has any single country, no matter how many national brands are combined. More than 90 breweries operate under the company's supervision, producing Heineken and a variety of popular national beers all over the world. The production of these beers accounts for sales in roughly 50 of Heineken's 150 foreign markets. The rest, including the American market, are reached through exports from the Netherlands. The production at the brewery built by Gerard Adriaan Heineken in Rotterdam has been relocated to larger, more modern facilities in Zoerterwoude, which has a production capacity of more than 5 million barrels (six million hectoliters) per year. The Heineken plant at 's-Hertogenbosch has a capacity of 3.4 million barrels (4 million hectoliters). Brewing in smaller quantities continues at the Amsterdam plant, which serves as more of a showcase brewery.

Traditionally, the Netherlands' second brand was Amstel, named for the river that

flows through Amsterdam. Since 1968, it has been part of the Heineken group, although separate brand identification is maintained. Today Heineken also owns the Murphy Brewery in Ireland and the Dreher Brewery in Italy.

After Heineken and Amstel, probably the best-known name on a label of a Dutch beer is Grolsch. In 1615, Jenneken Neerfelt, daughter of the owner of a local brewery in the town of Grol, married an enterprising young man named Peter Cuyper. An excellent brewer, Cuyper was, in 1677, appointed Guild Master over all the brewers in Grol (now Groenlo). He introduced the brewers to proper techniques and also taught following generations the secrets of brewing beer. Over the years, Grol beer (Grolsch) acquired an excellent reputation.

Among the other larger brewing companies whose labels are seen in the Netherlands are the likes of Brand in Wijle, Oranjeboom (Orange Tree) in Rotterdam and Drie Hoefijzers (Three Horseshoes) in Breda. There are also Belgian-style beers brewed by monks in the Netherlands, and American-style brew pubs began to make their appearance on the scene in the 1980s.

Clockwise from above: **Quite possibly the world's best known beer label; a label from Breda's Oranjeboom (Orange Tree); and a cozy Amsterdam cafe displaying the logo of the brand named for the city's main waterway.**

At right: Labels of Heineken's namesake brand, the most popular beer in the Netherlands, and the stout of the Van Vollenhoven subsidiary. The first label shown is from 1972, before the Zoerterwoude plant replaced the one in Rotterdam. Heineken attributes its distinctive flavor to the special Heineken A-yeast, developed more than a century ago by Dr Elion, a student of Dr Louis Pasteur. Since 1888, the Heineken A-yeast has been used to help maintain a consistent quality beer worldwide. Today the yeast is regularly shipped via air courier to the Heineken subsidiaries and affiliate breweries which brew the Heineken brand.

At right: Amstel, the Heineken company's second most popular brand, can be traced back to 1870 when the brewing company De Pesters, Kooy & Company was founded in Amsterdam. Several brands of beer are brewed under the Amstel umbrella, catering to a wide variety of tastes: Amstel, Amstel Gold, an Amstel Bock Bier, Oud Bruin (a sweet dark beer) and Amstel Light, a low-calorie beer. In 1988, after six years of extensive research, Heineken introduced its nonalcoholic brew, Buckler.

At right: Since 1898, Grolsch has bottled its beer in a unique bottle, a bottle with a porcelain wire stopper, also called a swingtop bottle. Although Grolsch is of course also obtainable in a variety of other types of cans and bottles, the swingtop bottle is the main type of consumer packaging. Like Heineken, Grolsch is responding to the growing Dutch and export market for alcohol-free (alcoholvrij) beer.

At right: The Dommelsche Brewery was founded by Willem Snieders at Dommeln in 1744. Dommelsche Pils is a Pilsen-style lager and Oud Bruin a dark ale, while Bokbier and Dominator are a bock and doppelbock, respectively, with an alcohol content in excess of six percent by volume. Dommelsche NA, by contrast, is a non-alcoholic brew.

At right: La Trappe is brewed at the Koningshoeven Trappist abbey in Tilburg. Similar to the more well-known abbey ales of Belgium, it is bottled in Belgium as the monks in Tilburg do not have their own bottling line.

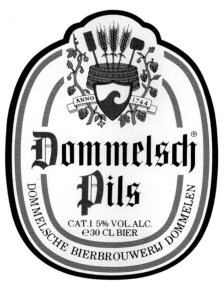

SCANDINAVIA

Above: Tuborg has been part of the Carlsberg Group since 1970, but maintains an independent brand identity and a separate brewing facility. The word *ol* is Danish for beer, and *hvidtol* is a wheat or 'white' beer with a long tradition in Denmark.

While the English word *ale* originated with the Norse word *aul* (as did the modern Danish and Norwegian *øl),* the tastes of contemporary Scandinavian beer drinkers runs not to ale, but to bottom-fermented beers. In fact, with the exception of Denmark, both the size and importance of brewing companies and the per capita consumption of beer are much less than elsewhere in northern Europe.

Lager beer may have been invented in Bavaria, but it was in Denmark that the first pure single strain of lager yeast–*sacharomyces carlsbergensis*–was developed. As the name suggests, it was named for the chemist for Scandinavia's largest brewing company–Carlsberg of Copenhagen. As the story goes, Emil Christian Hansen brought lager yeast from Germany in 1875 in a top hat, which he preserved by continuously re-filling with cold water. Once back in Copenhagen, he carefully bred the pure *sacharomyces carlsbergensis*, and today, the brewery modestly boasts 'probably the best lager in the world?'

The Carlsberg story begins with JC Jacobsen, born in 1811, the son of an already-established Danish brewer, Christen Jacobsen of Copenhagen. Jacobsen, aware of Denmark's poor reputation as a brewing nation, tried to teach his son a more scientific and systematic approach to the brewer's art by enrolling him at the newly established Copenhagen Technical University. In 1835, Christen Jacobsen died, leaving his 24-year-old son sole heir to one of Denmark's most advanced breweries. In keeping with his father's systematic approach, JC Jacobsen made several trips to Germany in order to learn more about the brewing industry. It was here that he became acquainted with bottom-fermented lager.

In 1845, Jacobsen acquired a piece of land in the Copenhagen suburb of Valby and built the first Carlsberg Brewery, which he named after his son Carl. Production of the first brew began on 10 November 1847, and this date is still celebrated today as Carlsberg's anniversary. In 1872, JC Jacobsen established a second brewery for his son Carl. This was inaugurated in 1881 as 'Ny Carlsberg' (New Carlsberg), as opposed to JC Jacobsen's own breweries which were called 'Gamie Carlsberg' (Old Carlsberg). JC Jacobsen died in 1887, and in 1906 Gamie Carlsberg and Ny Carlsberg were merged into a single entity, the Carlsberg Breweries.

Traditionally, Denmark's second biggest brewing company was Tuborg, founded in 1873. Relations between Tuborg and Carlsberg had always been generally good, and in 1970, as Denmark entered the European Common Market, the two merged into the Carlsberg Group. Tuborg retained its brand identity and continues to be brewed at its own plant in Copenhagen.

Emerging as Denmark's new second largest brewer is Ceres, of which Carlsberg is now a part owner. Ceres is based in Arhus and is allied with Thor Brewing as part of the Jutland Group, which has breweries in Hjorring, Randers and Horsens.

While beer and brewing are less important in the other nations of Scandinavia (Norway's first commercial brewery was founded in 1776), each does have a well-developed brewing industry and home market. The largest brewing companies in the their respective countries are Pripps in Gothenberg and Bromma in Sweden; Ringnes (part of the Noral Group) of Oslo, Norway; and Sinebrychoff (aka Koff), with plants in Helsinki, Tampere and Pori in Finland.

At right: Selected Carlsberg labels include the famous 'Elephant' brand, which celebrates the famous gate at the Copenhagen brewery. Elephant Beer is a high alcohol (7.5 percent by volume) premium lager with a strong following in Denmark and other markets. Pilsner is Carlsberg's biggest brand.

At right: Carlsberg brews Kongens Bryg, celebrating Holger Danske, the guardian of the Danish race, who resides in the vaults of Kronborg Castle in Elsinore, home of Carlsberg's Wiibroe subsidiary brewery. Giraf is a popular brand brewed at Odense by Albani. Founded in 1859, Albani is one of Denmark's oldest brewers. Aass (pronounced *orse*) in Dranmen is Norway's oldest brewery, founded in 1867.

At right: Ceres of Arhus in the Jutland region is Denmark's second biggest brewing company. Products include Christmas (Jule) beer and Paaske Hvidtol is a wheat beer brewed for Easter. The Faxe Bryggeri (brewery) is located in Fakse, south of Copenhagen.

At right: Ringnes export is the export version of Ringnes Pilsener Øl, the largest-selling beer in Norway. Norsk is the export version of Ringnes Zero Plus. Pripps of Gothenberg is Sweden's largest brewing company.

  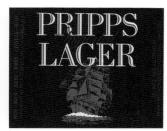

At right: Oy Hartwall was founded in 1884. Although its headquarters and bottling plant are in Helsinki, brewing takes place at other sites in Finland, such as Lappeenranta and Torino. Lapin Kulta, Hartwall's flagship export brand, is brewed at Torino, which is in Lapland, near the Swedish border. The Roman numerals represent the relative percentage of alcohol ranging from I (2.8 percent) to IVA (5.2 percent).

BELGIUM

In the world of beer and brewing, Belgium is a place apart. There is as large a range of beer styles in this small country as there is in all the rest of the world, and Belgium has more breweries per capita than in any other nation on earth. When the Belgian brewing industry bills the nation as a 'Beer Paradise,' it may actually be making an understatement. This variety of beer styles has generated a vast spectrum of label designs, from the staid labels of breweries run by Trappist monks, to the outlandish and whimsical labels of the microbreweries.

When it comes to Belgian beer, all of the superlatives apply. While absolute volume and per capita consumption are less, Belgian beer drinkers can make their choices from a dizzying variety and level of quality unheard of elsewhere. Until the North American microbrewery revolution, there were more brewing companies in Belgium than in the entire Western Hemisphere. These breweries range from those brewing the hugely popular Jupiler and Stella Artois brands, to tiny firms the size of North American microbreweries, that have been small for years, or even centuries.

In the region that is now modern Belgium, beer was originally brewed on private farms. Until the eleventh century, commercial beer was the prerogative of the abbeys, over a dozen of which are still brewing commercial quantities of beer. Later, brewing became a trade and beer brewers formed influential guilds to protect not only the producers, but their customers. The superb seventeenth century guild houses of Belgian brewers, which still stand on the spectacular Grand Place in Brussels, bear witness to the importance and wealth of the Belgian brewing industry.

Brewing in Belgium is still largely the work of skilled artisans. At the turn of the century, there were more than 3000 brewers. Indeed, at one time, Belgium even had more brewers than burgermeisters. Only 150 breweries remain active today, but many of them have gained an international reputation. Even though production equipment has been modernized, brewing techniques and regional recipes remain much the same as they were five centuries ago.

Today Belgium's two largest brewers—Jupiler and Stella Artois—are both part of the Interbrew Group. Founded in Jupille near Liege, the Jupiler Brewery dates back to 1853, while Artois in Leuven traces its roots to 1399.

While these two companies are both lager brewers, another important slice of the Belgian brewing world belongs to the abbey (abbage or abdij) beers, which are brewed by Trappist monks at 12 monasteries throughout the country. Abbey ales are a recognized brewing style, and the ales are extremely popular, representing a dynamic line of continuity in the Belgian brewing heritage. Monasteries evolved as brewing centers because for centuries, they were centers of literacy and study, art and science. They were also a refuge and resting place for pilgrims traveling to shrines or the Holy Land. Pilgrims

Above: This series of rare, vintage-dated 1941 labels from Gent's Huyghe Brewery was produced during the Nazi occupation.

Opposite: A refreshing glass of Belle-Vue Kriek, one of the delightful cherry beers indigenous to Belgium's Senne Valley, one of the most unusual beer-producing regions in the world *(see text, page 34).*

Left: The sixteenth-century facade of the Maison de Brasseurs (Guild Hall of the Brewers) on the Grand Place in Brussels.

Above: **Beer is Belgium's national beverage and indeed the cafés often advertise their beer selection in a bigger way than their own names. Taverne La Madeleine in Brussels features Stella Artois and Maes Pils, two of Belgium's leading lagers, but also has a more extensive beer list posted at the right of its neat picture window.**

Below: **A la Mort Subite (Sudden Death) is one of Brussels' best-known and best-loved fin-de-siècle beer halls. Brasserie Vossen brews Mort Subite beer which is named for a dice game played at the beer hall, not for the effects of the beer.**

Opposite: **The products brewed by the Trappist monks at the Abbey of Notre Dame of Scourmont near Chimay are among Belgium's most highly regarded abbey beers.**

who stayed for a night or two needed food and drink, so the monasteries brewed their own beer, made their own cheeses and baked bread, as some still do.

In much of Europe, the great era of monastic brewing came to an end when the abbeys were secularized by Napoleon or destroyed in the French Revolution. For the Belgian brewing industry, however, this was only a minor setback. After the Revolution, religious orders from France crossed the border and built new abbeys. The monks were also aware that, while other countries may have a more standardized approach to brewing practice, Belgium was a land of individualists. Each part of the country had its own variations in brewing techniques, resulting in beers that had a great variety of strengths and styles, each with its own bouquet, color and palate. Each monastery also developed its own brewing methods, and these techniques have been perfected in the twentieth century to create several distinct abbey styles of beer. Today monastery brews are still based on such a tradition. Many of these beers, though not all, are dark in color. All are made with top-fermenting yeast and so are, technically, speaking, ales.

The largest selling of the abbey beers are those from the Abbey of Notre Dame of Scourmont near Chimay, and are known by their familiar Chimay label. The other Trappist abbeys brewing beer include Notre Dame de la Paix (also at Chimay), Notre Dame d'Orval (Orval), Notre Dame de St Remy (Rochefort), Westmalle (Westmalle), St Sixtus (Westvleteven), St Benedictus (Achel), Notre Dame de Brialmont (Brial-

mont), Notre Dame de Clairefontaine (Clairefontaine), Notre Dame de Nazareth (Brecht) and Notre Dame de Soleilmont (Soleilmont).

While the tradition of monastic brewing has survived, prospered and continued to be an important influence, it is now only one of many elements in Belgium's brewing culture. Farmhouse breweries and microbreweries gave rise to some of today's specialties, and represent another fiercely independent Belgian traditions. Perhaps the most notable of these are the Lambic beers from the Lambic (or Lembeek) region, specifically the Senne Valley, in an area south of Brussels. Lambic beers are unique from nearly all other beers in the world in that they are produced with *neither* lager yeast nor ale yeast. They are spontaneously fermented with wild yeasts native only to that valley.

Some notable types of Lambics include Gueuze and unique fruit beers. The latter are brewed using fruits as a flavoring, just as other beers use hops to flavor the malt beverage. Most common fruit lambics are Kriek, made with cherries, and Frambozen (or Framboise), made with raspberries. Other versions use various types of berries or peaches.

The wealth of Belgian beer styles includes wheat beer (known as witbier in the province of Brabant, where it is made), Faro (a sugary gueuze) and Goudenband (brown ale), as well as nearly any type of beer that can be found elsewhere in the world.

Truly, Belgium is a world of wonderful beers in one of the smallest countries in Europe.

At right: The Brouwerij du Bocq in Purnode brews a wide variety of beers which it describes as the 'country beers' of the Ardennes and the Meuse River region. Triple Moine and Deugniet are described as the 'secret of long life.'

At right: The Belle-Vue brewery was established in the Senne Valley in 1913 by Philemon Vanden Stock, acquiring its name in 1927 when he brought the tenancy of the Cafe Belle-Vue in Anderlecht. Interbrew acquired the brewery in July 1991.

At right: Founded in 1791, the Bosteel's family brewery in Buggenhout has some phonetically interesting brand names.

At right: Located in the heart of Brussels, Cantillon produces lambics with amusing labels that celebrate the city, as well as the finer aspects of Belgian life.

At right: There are four types of Chimay Ale: the fruity Chimay Premiere (red on black), the much drier Chimay CinqCents (white), the peppery Chimay Grand Reserve (gold) and the Chimay (blue).

At right: La Chouffe in Achouffe near Bastogne is a microbrewery founded in 1982 by Pierre Gobron and Christian Bauweraerts. *Chouffes* are legendary mute gnomes who drink from the River Decrogne to gain the ability to speak. Gobron and Bauweraerts leave the materials for their beer in their brewhouse overnight and the *chouffes* do the brewing.

At right: Corsendonk Abbey in Oud-Turnhout was founded by Maria van Gelre, youngest daughter of the Duke of Brabant.

Also at right: The Crombe Brewery in Zottegem has been brewing–originally as an abbey brewery–since 1806. Duke Egmont, a general for Charles V, was beheaded in Brussels in 1568.

At right: De Dolle is a microbrewery that opened in Esen in 1980 with whimsical labels that are highly prized by collectors. Boskeun (Easter Bunny) is, as the name suggests, a seasonal beer with varying degrees of honey in the aroma. Stille Nacht (Silent Night) is a Christmas beer.

At right: The Dubuisson Brewery in Ripaix was founded in 1769 and has been brewing Bush (Scaldis) since 1933.

At right: The Gouden Boom (Golden Tree) Brewery in Bruges brews a white wheat beer, as well as abbey-style Steenbrugge.

Also at right: In 1989, Jean Pierre Eloir founded his brewery of the same name at Montignies. His abbey-style and the name pays tribute to the Abbaye des Rocs.

At right and below right: The devilishly colorful labels of the popular Hopdvel (Hop Devil) Brewery in Gent are contrasted with the more conventional labels of the Huyghe Brewery, also in Gent.

At right: Beer has been brewed in Hoegaarden since well before the first written mention of a brewery in 1318. Begarden monks began brewing the Hoegaarden Witbier (White Beer) in 1445. This wheat beer was popular throughout Belgium for five centuries, but competition from the mass market lagers caused the last brewery's closure in 1957. Hoegaardiers felt the need to revive their tradition, and in 1965 Pieter Celis again started to brew the naturally cloudy white beer. Since 1978, the De Kluis Brewery has perfected other beers, such as the brown Benedict, the clearer Grand Cru, the spicy Forbidden Fruit and the flowery Julius.

In 1992, Pieter Celis emigrated to the United States, where he began brewing his critically acclaimed Celis White, a witbier that has been very favorably compared to Hoegaarden.

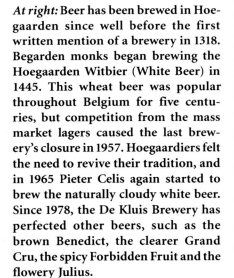

At right: The Abbey at Grimbergen, near Brussels, has one of the handful of abbey breweries where the monks are not Trappists. The Abbey was founded in 1128, the first of the Norbertine order. Grimbergen Double is a deep red, top-fermented beer with a mild, fruity flavor.

At far right: The Piedboeuf family, who founded Jupiler in 1853, has been in Jupille, since 1445. Launched in 1966, Jupiler Lager from Jupille is Belgium's largest selling brand.

At right: The Abbey of Leffe, near Dinant was founded in 1152 by the Premontratesian Order. Since 1954, Leffe's St Guibert Brewery at Mont St Guibert has produced the abbey-style beers such as leffe Blonde, Radieuse, Triple, Brune and Vieux Temps Amber.

At right: Liefman's Brewery in Oudenburg dates to 1679, but the Abbey of St Arnoldus was probably brewing beer as early as 1084. Liefman's produces both fruit ales and a brown ale (*goudenband*).

At right: Lindeman's farmhouse brewery in Vlezenbeek produces both gueuze and fruit lambics. These wonderfully art nouveau labels were designed by Charles Finkel, whose firm, Merchant du Vin, imports Lindeman's beers into the United States.

At right: Loburg was launched in 1977 as a 'premium' variation on Stella Artois Lager.

Also at right: Placide Louwaege stopped farming in 1877 and moved to Kortemark to buy one of the existing breweries, where he brewed a lager called Akila (eagle). Hapkin is a pale ale whose recipe is said to have been invented at the Abbey of Ter Duinen, by request of the Count of Flanders, Hapkin-with-the-Axe.

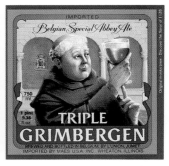

At right: It was in 1880 that Egide Maes (pronounced *marse)* purchased the St Michael Brewery in Waarloos and began brewing the popular Pilsen-style lager that bears his name.

Also at right: A label from abbey-style ales from the Maredsous Brewery in Denee.

Below: Adriaan Geerkens began brewing at his inn at Bocholt in 1758. His granddaughter Isabella married Theodorus Martens in 1823 and their son Frans was an important factor in developing what would evolve into today's Martens Brewery. Still family-owned, the brewery went through a great expansion after World War II, and today exports both top- and bottom-fermented beer throughout Europe and the world. The Sezoens (Seasons) ale–on whose label winter hands a beer to summer–was awarded the Gold Medal of the World Beer Selection of Brussels in 1991.

At right (two rows): Among the most well-known secular Belgian ales, is the famous Duvel beer, brewed by the Moortgat family at Breendonk. The brewery was founded in 1871 by Jan Leonart Moortgat, and under the second generation of brewers, Victor and Albert, the brewery started to develop new products, including a Brabant witbier called Steendonk. Today Moortgat also brews several Pilsen-style lagers: Bel, Godefroy, Silver and Wonder.

At right: The Trappist monks at the Abbaye Notre Dame de St Remy at Rochefort have been brewing since 1595, but it has only been in the last quarter of the twentieth century that their unique ales have become known outside the province of Namur.

At right: Alexander Rodenbach first began brewing at Roeselare in the province of West Flanders in 1836. The uniquely fruity Rodenbach ales are among the only beers in the world still aged in wooden tuns as pictured on the Grand Cru label.

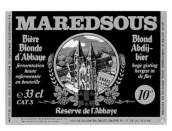

At right and below: In 1880, the birth of a son inspired a man named De Splenter to set up a brewery. By the period between the two World Wars, the De Splenter Brewery was regularly brewing some 50 barrels (60 hectoliters) of ale a week. In 1968, Yvan De Splenter renamed the enterprise Brouwerij Riva and built an ultra modern brewery. By 1980, Riva ales were already being exported, mainly to Europe, but also to North America. Vondel Ale is named for Joost van den Vondel, the most famous Dutch writer of the Golden Age. Lucifer, named after Vondel's best-known work, is a fiery, intense ale. Dentergem's White Ale is a typical witbier, brewed according to a proven recipe in the region of the River Lys. Aromas of selected herbs sweeten the taste and character.

In 1070, a group of Benedictine monks from Calabria, Italy, established an abbey in the Golden Valley *(val d'or)*, which has come to be known as Orval. During the twelfth century, at the request of Count Albert of Chiny (St Bernard of Clairvaux), the Church sent monks from Trois-Fontaines. True to Cistercian tradition, these monks from the Champagne region built their abbey along the Roman road between Reims and Trier (Treves).

The little pond, clear and cold, next to the portal of Our Lady's church, owes its name to the charming legend that is immortalized by the illustration on the label of Orval beer. In the eleventh century, the suzeraine of the region was Countess Matilda, Duchess of Tuscany and Godfrey of Bouillon's aunt. In about 1076, she wished to see the courageous settlers from Calabria. Sitting at the edge of the spring, which was providing water to the monastery, she accidentally dropped her wedding ring into the water. This ring was a keepsake of her late husband. Overcome with its loss, the Countess ardently beseeched the Virgin Mary. Suddenly, a trout rising out of the water returned the precious ring to her. Filled with awe at what had just happened, the Countess cried out, 'Why, this is truly a "val d'or"!'

Sacked and plundered during the seventeenth century, rebuilt, enlarged and improved by its inhabitants, the abbey was then bombarded in the eighteenth century by General Loison. It was in 1926 that the Abbaye d'Orval rose again from its ruins, thanks to the initiative of Dom Marie-Albert Van der Cruyssen. In 1948, after World War II, the present abbey was completed. Today some 40 monks live and work at the Abbaye d'Orval, brewing their distinctive beer.

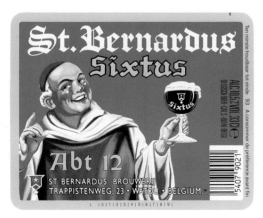

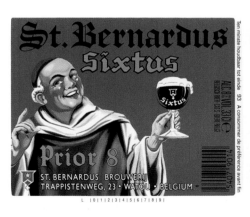

Above: The St Bernadus Brewery is located in Watou in Flanders in the heart of the famous Popering hop-growing district. For three generations, the Claus family has brewed exclusively under the license of the tiny St Sixtus Abbey, using the Abbey recipe and brewing techniques.

At right and below: The Artois Brewery dates to the House of Den Horen, an inn in Leuven which first brewed its own beer in 1366, and from 1537 sold its products to the University of Leuven (founded in 1425). Den Horen had many owners before Sebastien Artois bought it in 1717. He had been an apprentice there, earning the title of master brewer in 1708, and his many descendants included several master brewers.

It was his grandson, Leonard, who managed a vigorous expansion, buying two neighboring breweries on the quays of the 'new' Leuven-Rupel Canal: the Fransche Kroon in 1787 and the Prins Karel in 1793. The Den Horen Artois Brewery quickly became one of the largest in the Austro-Hungarian Empire, brewing some 63,000 barrels (71,000 hectoliters) per year. Artois 'bock' beer was launched in 1892. It was a low-fermentation Pilsen-style lager that was the father of today's Stella Artois.

Artois Brewery Company was incorporated in 1901, and soon after, Professor Verhelst, director of the Academy of Brewing at Leuven University, became its managing director and played a key role in its development and survival through two World Wars. Stella Artois, named after the Christmas star, was a 'special occasion' beer launched in 1926. Today, Stella Artois is part of the Interbrew Group.

At right and below right: The St Jozef Brewery in Opittern-Bree produces its own range of beers–from lager to kriek–as well as license-brewed products. The brewery traces it roots to 1807.

At right: The Brasserie de Silly, at Silly west of Brussels, has been a family microbrewery since 1848.

Also at right: St Sebastiaan is brewed by the Sterkens-Meer Brewery.

Also at right: The piercing eyes of Hendrik himself glower out from the label of Straffe Hendrik, brewed in Brugge by the Straffe Hendrik family since 1856.

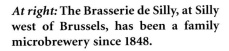

At right (two rows): In 1887, the brewery in Itterbeek in the Senne Valley known as the 'Little Mole' was taken over by Paul Walravens, whose daughter married Fraz Timmermans in 1911. Their grandsons Raoul and Jacques van Custem are the current owners of the Timmermans Brewery. As with other breweries in the Senne, Timmermans brews a wide variety of lambics, including gueuze, kriek (cherry), framboise (raspberry), cassis (black current) and peche (peach).

At right (two rows): De Troch Brewery in Ternat-Wambeek brews the Chapeu brand of lambics that include a wider variety of fruits than a typical lambic brewer, such as Timmermans *(above).* These include such fruits as bananas, which are clearly not native to Belgium. The labels have a very appealing design.

At right (two rows): The Vander Linden Brewery produces a variety of products, from its flagship Vieux Foudre to the wickedly intriguing Biere du Diable (Devil's Brew).

At right: The labels of Brouwerij Leroy in Boezinge include brand names in both English (Old Musketeer) and German (Sasbräu). 'Yperman' is a humorous reference to the Flemish city of Ypres.

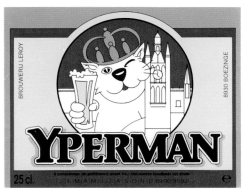

At right: The Brasserie à Vapeur ('Steam Brewery') at Pipaix in the province of Hainaut is justifiably proud of its steam engine. Saison de Pipaix is a highly-spiced seasonal beer.

At right (two rows): The Vieille Villers Brewery at Puurs produces a variety of uniquely Belgian styles, from Liezelse, a witbier, to Loo, an abbey-style beer.

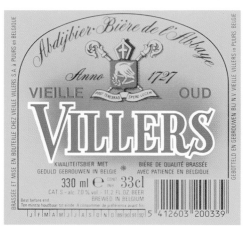

GERMANY

Above and below: **Promoting the products of Munich's graphically well-identified Spaten brand.**

Even more than in Belgium, the national drink of Germany is beer. In terms of absolute production, Germany ranks second only to the United States. Even before unification, West Germany by itself was well ahead of third-place Britain. Two out of every five breweries in the world are located in Germany.

With nearly 1500 breweries–more than in all the world outside Europe combined–Germany has witnessed the evolution of a very robust industry. With strong brewing companies in every region and state, Germany has no single dominant brand as do France, the Netherlands and Denmark. Dortmund is Germany's largest brewing city, with the Dortmunder Actien Bräuerei (DAB) and the rival Dortmunder Union Bräuerei (DUB) located there.

The brewing tradition of Dortmund began in 1293 and progressed into the nineteenth century when Dortmunder bottom-fermented beers became popular. Dortmunder lagers are traditionally full bodied but not quite as sweet as the beers of Munich and not as dry as a pilsner. This style evolved when they began transporting beer to other markets across the continent. In order to withstand the rigors of travel, Dortmund brewers produced a beer that was well hopped and slightly higher in alcohol.

The Dortmunder Union Bräuerei (DUB) was formed in 1873 by the merger of several small breweries, and has been ranked among the top 10 German breweries since 1939. Because of its location in the heavily bombed industrial Ruhr, the brewery was 75 percent destroyed in World War II. It was rebuilt and enjoyed continuous growth until 1972, when it merged with two other brewing groups and became the Dortmunder Union Schultheiss Bräuerei. DUB is now part of Bräu und Brunnen AG, the largest beverage group in Germany. The Bräu and Brunnen Brewing and Natural Springs represents a thriving beverage group with annual beer sales of 5.3 million barrels (6.3 million hectoliters) and 4.5 million barrels (5.3 million hectoliters) in nonalcoholic beverages.

The leading breweries in Bräu und Brunnen are: DUB; Dortmunder Ritter, located in Dortmund; Heidelberger Schlossguell Bräuerei, (home of the famous Valentins Weizen Beer) in Heidelberg; Schultheiss Bräuerei, the largest brewery in Berlin; and Einbecker Bräu Haus in Einbeck, the oldest bock beer brewery in Germany.

Another major holding group is the Maerz Group, which formed around the Erste Kulmbacher Union (EKU) brewery in the 1980s. Today it also owns Bavaria St Pauli of Hamburg (not to be confused with St Pauli of Bremen or any brewery actually *in* Bavaria), as well as Auberg, Eichbaum, Frankenthaler, Henninger and Tucher.

The Beck's label that is sent forth to the world from the port city of Bremen is perhaps the biggest German export beer, and the Bitburger label seems to dominate the Rhineland.

When it comes to superlatives, however, the state of Bavaria is to beer everything that its reputation implies. When it comes to

Above: The mecca of beer lovers is Munich's enormous Hofbräuhaus, the largest and most famous beer hall in the world.

Left: A selection of Deibels altbiers from Issum, the city that is noted for brewing altbiers or 'beers in the old style.' This translates to the use of top-fermenting (ale type) yeast rather than the more common bottom-fermenting (lager type) yeast.

beer, Bavaria is to Germany what Germany is to the world. A third of the world's breweries and 70 percent of Germany's breweries are in Bavaria, with breweries located in nearly every village.

Bavaria's capital, Munich, is home to six of Germany's legendary brewing companies: Augustiner, Löwenbräu, Hacker-Pschorr, Paulaner, Spaten-Franzenkaner and Hofbräuhaus, whose Munich beer hall of the same name is the largest and most famous drinking establishment in the world.

With its size, the German brewing industry also offers a variety of brewing styles. Lagers are omnipresent, with Munich, Dortmund and Cologne (Koln) all having their own indigenous variations. Dusseldorf, a modern industrial city, is known as the home of alt bier. Alt beer, which literally means 'beer in the old style,' is brewed with top-fermenting (ale-type) yeast as all beers were before the lager revolution of the nineteenth century. Weiss beers (wheat beers) also predate lagers and are today brewed throughout Germany with specific styles indigenous to northern Germany, Bavaria and especially Berlin, where Berliner-Weisse is the city's trademark beer.

As with many of North America's microbreweries, many German brewers offer a variety of styles, with most major brewers having light lagers (helles), dark lagers (dunkels), seasonal beers, double bocks (doppelbocks) and wheat beers.

The labels are as varied as the beers, but the national style seems to incorporate white and silver with a bit of blue or red, a look that conveys a sense of both cleanliness and precision. There are also local insignias, such as Berlin's bear and the blue and white of the Bavarian flag, that are used by Löwenbräu and several other Munich brewers.

Above: **A group of happy tipplers from Bitburg, home of the well-known Rhineland 'pils' of the same name.**

Left: **With roots dating back to medieval monastic breweries, Munich's Fraziskaner merged with Spaten in 1922, but the brand identification remains clear.**

Facing page: **A dramatically lit bottle of Löwenbräu's 'Special Export' an export version of the Munich brewer's well-known helles pils. The Löwenbräu export strategy excludes Greece, Sweden, Britain, Canada and the United States, where domestic brewers produce an approximation of the Munich beer under license.**

At right: The labels of Alpirsbachor Klosterbräu from Alpirsbach in the Black Forest celebrate the brewery's monastic heritage, which dates back to 1095 and the reign of Pope Urban II.

At right: The present Ayinger Brewery traces its roots to 1878 when the Bavarian village of Aying had its first tavern brewery. Brewmaster Franz Insekammer is the sixth generation of his family to preside over the kettles at Ayinger.

At right: The city-state of Bremen has been an important seaport since the days of the Hanseatic League more than 600 years ago. With this in mind, it is little wonder that the lagers of Bräuerei Beck & Company are Germany's leading export brand. These familiar red labels are found not only throughout Europe but on every continent.

Also at right: The Berliner Kindl (Child of Berlin) Brewery was established in 1872 and is Berlin's largest. Its labels pay tribute to Berlin's symbolic animal (Barenpils) and to Frederich the Great (Rex Pils).

At right: The labels and signage of Bitburger Bräuerei Theobold Simon are a ubiquitous sight in the valley of the Rhine and are known in 24 countries throughout Europe, as well as in North America and the Far East.

The brewery was founded at Bitburg in 1817 by Johann Peter Wallenborn to produce alt beer for his own pub. In 1876, his grandson Theobold Simon began an aggressive marketing plan, and in 1884 he switched from alt to lager and Bitburger Pils was born.

The brewery reached the 840,000-barrel (one-million-hectoliter) production level in 1973 and doubled that output in the next 10 years, making it one of Germany's leading national brands.

At right (three rows): 'Diebels, das freundliche (friendly) Alt' reads the slogan for Germany's largest selling alt beer, which is brewed in the small town of Issum on the lower Rhine near Dusseldorf. Diebels has also marketed a highly successful nonalcoholic alt beer, Issumr Alkoholfrei, since 1987, and a light beer, Diebels Light, since April 1992. Josef Diebels wrote to the mayor of Issum on 31 August 1877 requesting permission to start a brewery. The rest is history. In 1981, Diebels reached an annual production of 840,000 barrels (one million hectoliters) of beer, and in 1982 Diebels Alt reached the pinnacle of the alt beer market. Today Dr Paul Boesken-Diebels, a great-grandson of the brewery's founder, is the CEO.

At right: A selection of labels from some of the major breweries in Dortmund, Germany's premiere brewing city: Dortmunder Actien Bräuerei (DAB), Dortmunder Kronen and Dortmunder Stifts. The Stifts Clarissen Bräu is in the style brewed in the Middle Ages at the Clarissen Monastery in Horde, a suburb of Dortmund.

At right and on facing page: Dortmunder Union Bräuerei (DUB) is the largest brewery in Germany's major brewing city of Dortmund. The 'Union' in the name indicates the 1873 merger of a dozen Dortmund breweries. DUB is now part of the Bräu und Brunnen Group, Germany's leading beverage company.

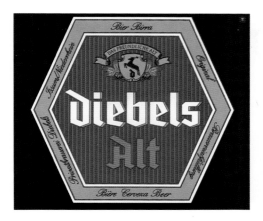

At right: Dinkelacker, Stuttgart's leading brewery, was founded by Carl Dinkelacker in 1888. The product line includes Cluss, a Keller-style lager, and Leicht, a low-calorie beer introduced in 1990.

At right and below: The Eichbaum (Oak Tree) Brewery was founded in Mannheim in 1679 and began brewing lagers in 1845. Destroyed in World War II, the brewery did not really get back on its feet again for 20 years, but by 1990 it had surpassed the 840,000-barrel (one-million-hectoliter) level.

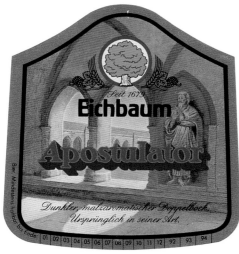

Also at right: Einbecker, which traces its roots back to the fourteenth century, is now part of the Bräu und Brunnen Group.

At right (two rows): The Erste Kulmbacher Union (EKU) is an amalgam of smaller breweries in the Kulmbach area that joined together in 1872 to brew Echt Kulmbacher Pils, which is still the EKU flagship beer. EKU acquired Henninger of Frankfurt in 1987, and today both are part of the Maerz Group.

At right (two rows): The Feldschlosschen Brewery at Bräunschweig (Brunswick) dates back to 1888. The company prides itself on its sports sponsorships. *(see also page 60).*

At right: The Felsenkeller Herford Brewery was founded by Georg Uekermann in 1878.

Also at right: Frankenheim, like many other Dusseldorf brewers, produces alt beer.

At right: The Gatzweiler family has been brewing alt beer since 1313, and operated the Zum Schlussel Haus Bräuerei (a brewpub) in Dusseldorf from 1937 to 1944 when it was destroyed in World War II. Zum Schlussel was rebuilt after the war and was augmented by the construction of a large, modern brewery in 1963. The traditional alt beer line was expanded in 1988 by the introduction of the non-alcoholic alt Gatz Alkoholfrei.

At right: In 1526, a brewer named Cord Broyhan brewed his first beer in Hannover. Two decades later, the Hannover Brewers Guild (Gilde) was founded, taking as its symbol a seal with Broyhan's initial. The Guild's brewery evolved over the centuries, and in 1968, it took over the 114-year-old Lindener Aktien-Bräuerei. The resulting entity was known as Lindener-Gilde until 1988 when the name of the newer entity was dropped from all but the labels.

At right (two rows): Heylands Bräuerei in Aschaffenburg dates from 1631 and has a range of label styles that features the city's landmark schloss.

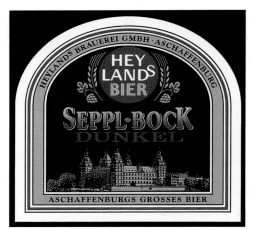

At right (three rows): One of Frankfurt's best-known brewing companies, Henninger has a strong market presence in the Mediterranean area. The company was begun in 1869 by Christian Henninger, and acquired by EKU in 1987. The Henninger labels retain a separate marketing identity.

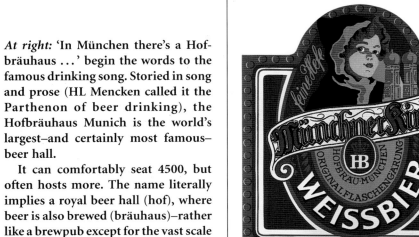

At right: 'In München there's a Hofbräuhaus ...' begin the words to the famous drinking song. Storied in song and prose (HL Mencken called it the Parthenon of beer drinking), the Hofbräuhaus Munich is the world's largest–and certainly most famous–beer hall.

It can comfortably seat 4500, but often hosts more. The name literally implies a royal beer hall (hof), where beer is also brewed (bräuhaus)–rather like a brewpub except for the vast scale and imperial overtones.

Today however, the HB lagers are brewed off site, but the beer hall remains as perhaps the top tourist attraction in the city that likes to think of itself as the world capital of beer drinking.

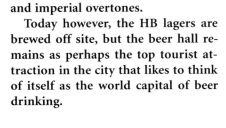

At right: Holsten was founded in 1879 and began brewing a year later at Altona (now part of Hamburg). By 1952, brewing plants at Hamburg, Kiel and Neumunster had exceeded 250,000 barrels (297,000 hectoliters). By the 1990s, Holsten was brewing over 700,000 (833,000 hectoliters) annually.

At right (two rows): Established in 1718, Kaiserdom is world famous for its Rauchbier, but the brewery also makes many of the other German beer styles as well.

Also at right: Konig-Pilsener is brewed at a family-operated brewery in Duisburg near Dusseldorf.

At right: The Krombacher Bräuerei Bernhard Schadeberg is based in Kreuztal-Krombach in North Rhine-Westphalia, between the Sieger and Sauer regions, where it brews Krombacher Pils.

At right: the Lauterbacher Burgbräuerei was founded in 1527 at Lauterbach in Hess. Under the label of the rooster, Lauterbacher also distributes the beers of Auerhahnbräu Schlitz. The latter uses the white on brown script for the word Schlitz in a fashion that is reminiscent of the once-popular American brand founded by Joseph Schlitz in Milwaukee in 1856. However, the Hessen Schlitz predates the Milwaukee Schlitz by 271 years.

This page: Lowenbräu *(loven-broy* or Lion's Brew) in Munich brews what may be the German beer with the most widely known label in the world. Beck's in Bremen may export more beer, but Löwenbräu is license-brewed in Britain, Japan, the United States and other major beer-drinking countries. Today one of Munich's Big Six, Löwenbräu began in 1383 as a Munich brewpub called Zum Lowen and evolved into a major lager brewery between 1826 and 1855.

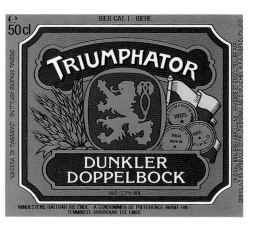

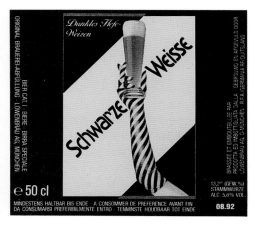

At right: The Bräuerei zur Malzmuhle (Malt Mill) in Cologne brews a low-alcohol lager called Kochsches Malzbier, as well as Muhlen Kolsch (The Windmill of Cologne) beers.

At right (two rows): One of Munich's Big Six, Paulaner dates back to the first beer brewed in 1631 by the monks of the order of St Francis of Paula. The monks sold their beer to the public after 1780, but the brewery became a secular lager brewery early in the nineteenth century. Today it incorporates Thomas Bräu, and is Munich's largest brewery, with an annual production approaching 1.6 million barrels (1.9 hectoliters).

At right: Sachsische Bräu Union (SBU) in Dresden was one of the largest government-owned brewing companies in the old East Germany (DDR). Today with an infusion of technical expertise from Holsten in Hamburg, SBU is gearing up for the market economy. Shown here are post-unification labels introduced after 1990. See page 55 for labels of the Feldschlosschen and Felsenkeller breweries which had also existed in *western* Germany.

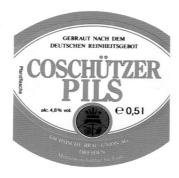  

At right: The Franz Joseph Sailer (Rauchenfels) Bräuerei in Marktoberdorf produces hefeweiss, as well as the unique steinbiere (stone-brewed beer). For centuries, heated stones were the only method of heating large quantities of liquid. Such beers were most often produced in the Alpine region near quarries. When large breweries were built in the nineteenth century, the tedious practice became forgotten until Rauchenfels revised it.

At right: The familiar St Pauli girl graces what are probably the most widely noticed German export beer labels.

Also at right: The Bräuerei Schlosser is located in the heart of Dusseldorf's altstadt ('old city'), the mecca for those interested in German altbier. Schlosser is now part of the Dortmunder Union (DUB) Group.

At right: During the seventeenth and eighteenth centuries, weiss beer had been tremendously popular in Germany. However, when Georg Schneider took over the Weiss Hofbräuhaus in Munich in 1872, weiss beer had been suffering a dramatic loss of market share to lager. Schneider sought to re-establish the popularity of the style in Bavaria, and succeeded. In 1928, the old weissbräuhaus in Kelheim on the Danube was also acquired. The finest weiss beer breweries of the seventeenth and eighteenth centuries were under common management.

At right (three rows): Some of the many and varied labels of Stuttgart's Schwaben Bräu Robert Leicht AG. Today's modern facility evolved from the first beer brewed in 1878 by Robert Leicht at his gasthof (guest house) called Ochsen.

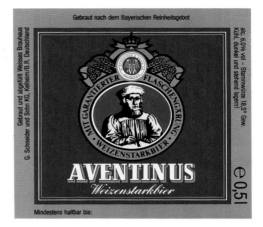

This page: The beers of Spaten-Franziskaner represent the results of the 1922 merger of Gabriel Sedlmayr's Spaten (spade) Brewery and the Franziskaner (Franciscan) Brewery which was originally a monastic brewery. The result is now one of Munich's Big Six brewing companies. Although the company traces its beginning to 1397, Spaten's true turning point occurred in the early nineteenth century when Gabriel Sedlmayr became the first major Munich brewer to begin brewing large quantities of lager.

As such, Sedlmayr played a pivotal role in the lager revolution and the development of the Munich style of lager. Today products include Spaten lagers and Franziskaner weiss beers.

At right: The labels of VEB Sternburg in Leipzig are examples of those used by the government-owned breweries in Eastern Germany in the years before reunification.

Also at right: The Tucher Brewery in Nürnberg in northern Bavaria dates from 1672.

At right: The Wolters family brewery had been around for over 200 years when the Duke of Brunswick made it his Hofbräuhaus by ducal warrant in the nineteenth century.

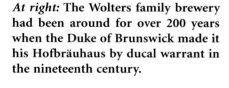

Also at right: The Wurzburger Hofbräuhaus was established in Wurzburg, northern Bavaria, in 1643. These labels include fanciful designs for seasonal beers.

At right: Zittauer Hell, a pale lager brewed in Zittau by what used to be the East German state-owned Societats-Bräuerei. These charming label predate German reunification.

AUSTRIA AND SWITZERLAND

Above: **Early labels and advertising materials from Vienna's Ottakringer Bräuerei.**

Right: **A colorful views of the Adambräuerei facility at Innsbruck in 1910.**

Facing page: **The Streiriche Group's Gösser has one of the most distinct labels in Austria.**

Brewing began in Austria well over a thousand years ago, and was well established by the seventeenth century. The Vienna style of lager was first brewed by Anton Dreher at Schwechat near Vienna in the 1840s.

Lager accounts for well over 90 percent of the beer brewed and marketed in the world (outside England). Specifically, it is a pale, clear beer fermented with bottom-fermenting yeast at nearly freezing temperatures. The fermentation period is also longer than that for ale and hence the name, which is German meaning 'to store.' Lager had its origins in the heart of central Europe in an area that I like to call the Golden Triangle. This triangle is so named because of the golden color of lager itself and because of the success that brewers had with this product when it was first developed for widespread commercial sale in the early to middle nineteenth century. The corners of the Triangle lie in Munich, Prague and Vienna, the capitals, respectively, of Bavaria (a state of the German republic), Bohemia (Czechoslovakia) and Austria.

As with Germany, but distinctly unlike France, the Netherlands and Denmark, Austria has no dominant national brand, but rather several well established regional brands. These brewers are in turn part of larger marketing groups. The biggest is the Osterreichische Bräu Aktiengesellschaft (Austrian Brew Corporation) or BräuAG, with headquarters at Linz in northern Austria between Vienna and Salzburg. The second largest is the Steirische Bräuindustrie Aktiengesellschaft (Styrian Brew Industry Corporation), which is headquartered at Graz in the province of Steirmark (Styria) in southern Austria. These groups are respectively represented herein by Kaltenhausen in Salzburg and Gösser in Göss, whose distinctive label uses the green and white colors of the Steirmark flag. There are also many smaller local brewers in Vienna and throughout Austria.

Like Germany and Austria, Switzerland is a nation of regional breweries rather than one dominant national brand, as is the case in countries such as the Netherlands and Denmark.

Legend has it that St Gall—an Irish monk whose name enters the literature as one of the many patron saints of brewing—founded Switzerland's first brewery in the seventh century near the present-day city of St Gallen.

St Gallen still has a major brewery—Schutzengarten AG on St Jakostrasse—as do Basel (Warteck AG), Bern (Gurten AG), Chur (Calanda), Fribourg (Sibra), Luzern (Eichhof) and Winterthur (Haldengut). Zurich has two major brewers, Hürlimann and Löwenbräu Zurich, but the nation's largest is Feldschlosschen in Rheinfelden.

At right: The Adambräuerei labels feature the conical dome of Windegg Castle at Wilten, near Innsbruck, which Josef Adam transformed into a brewery in 1825. The old Wilten coat-of-arms has been retained in the firm's emblem. In 1917, a group of 38 Innsbruck innkeepers formed a cooperative and bought Adambräu in order to supply their own inns.

At right: The BräuAG Group is Austria's largest brewing organization. Brands include Kaiser, Schützen and Zipfer *(see below)*.

At right: Founded in 1475 and 1710, respectively, Hofbräu Kalten hausen near Salzburg and Wieselburger in Wieselburg are also part of BräAG. The products are generally pale lagers, with the except of Doppel Malz, which is a dark double bock, and Edelweiss, which is a weiss (wheat) beer.

At right: Vienna's own premier brewery is Ottakringer Bräuerei HarmerAG, which was founded in 1837 just as' the lager revolution was about to change the course of brewing history. Today the brewery's beers are marketed under the Gold Fassl brand.

Also at right: Founded in the city of Laa on the Thaya in 1454, the Hubertus Bräu labels of the Kuehtreiber Brewery feature the stag of Saint Hubert.

This page: The Steirische (Styrian) Group includes Puntigamer and Reininghaus of Graz, as well as the well-known Gösser Bräuerei at Göss. Gösser dates to 1459 when it was founded as a monastic brewery. The brewery was acquired by Max Kober in 1860, and from that time it evolved as one of Austria's most widely distributed brands.

At right: Vereinigte Kärntner BräuereinAG, the Villacher Bräuerei, was founded in 1858 in Villach, in the Tyrol midway between Innsbruck and Graz.

Villacher's Biercartoons, printed on coasters, received first place in their category in an international beer label competition in 1992.

At right: With labels bearing the distinctive long-tongued bear of Switzerland's capital canton, Gurten has been brewing in Wabern near Bern since Johann Juker first set up shop here in 1874. The labels also feature the local glee club and scenes that promote tourism.

At right: Calanda Haldengut traces its heritage to the Ernst family brewery in Winterthur in the early nineteenth century, but Johann Georg Schoolhorn, who entered the picture in 1875, is remembered as the man who put the brewery on the map, and William Tell on the label.

At right: These Albani Bräu labels from Haldengut in Winterthur have an engaging, almost medieval quality.

At right (two rows): **Hürlimann** was founded in 1836 and has been brewing on the same site since 1866. It is Zurich's largest brewing company.

Also at right: The Löwenbräu (Lion's Brew) Brewery in Zurch is occasionally confused with the more well-known Lowenbräu Brewery in Munich. The two are quite separate and the labels and colors quite different—except, of course, for the lion!

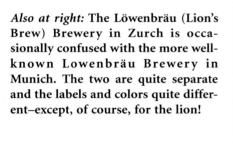

At right: St Gall may have first brewed beer at St Gallen in the seventh century, but Bräuerei Schutzengarten, the town brewery, dates to 1779. Schutzengarten features the saint on one of its labels and a view of the brewery in the nineteenth century on its Festbier label. The company also brews Birell, a popular nonalcoholic beer.

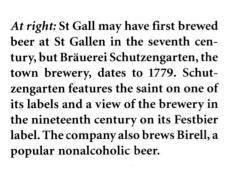

FRANCE

Above: In Adelshoffen's 1930s posters, Strasbourg's skyline and the Alsacian lifestyle were implicit.

Right: Checking the big copper kettles at Schiltigheim in the Alsace.

There is no other nation on earth where wine and the art of wine-making are elevated to such a lofty level of importance. French cuisine is the *haute* of *haute cuisine*, and French wine is inextricably linked with French cuisine. Against this backdrop, it would seem that beer would have little place. However, quite the opposite is true.

The French drink more wine than beer, but they drink far more beer per capita than the English, Germans or Americans drink wine. Americans drink less than one liter of wine for every 10 liters of beer. In Britain, the ratio is slightly more than one to 10, and in Germany—a nation with its own wine industry—the ratio is one to two. The French, on the other hand, drink four liters of beer for every seven liters of wine.

As with French cuisine and French viticulture, French beers are brewed with care and attention to the fine subtleties of flavor. Like French wines, French beers are carefully designed to accompany specific foods, and they succeed superbly. As Michael Jackson so aptly pointed out, the word *brasserie*, which implies a typical Parisian *café*, actually means *brewery*. What do Parisians typically drink in their brasseries? *Bière.*

The Alsace region is France's great brewing center, and its principal city, Strasbourg, is home to Brasseries Kronenbourg (BSN), which is by far the largest brewery in the country and the maker of France's most important export beer. The company also, ironically, brews more beer than any brewing company in Germany.

Kronenbourg was born in Strasbourg in June 1664, within a few yards of the old custom house on the banks of the Ill River, when Jerome Hatt, a newly certified master brewer, had just married and had affixed his seal to the first barrel of beer produced in his brewery, Brasserie du Canon. Today, Kronenbourg is Europe's largest selling bottled beer, with over 17 million barrels (20 million hectoliters) sold in 80 countries around the world annually.

The second biggest brewer in the Alsace—and the third largest in France—is the Fischer Group in Schiltigheim, which dates back to 1821 and includes Brasserie du Pecheur and Grande Brasserie Alsacienne d'Adelschoffen. Their Fischer brand is nearly as well known in some export markets as Kronenbourg.

Another important beer-producing area is centered around the city of Lille in the north in the Pas-de-Calais region, adjacent to the great brewing regions of Belgium. As in Belgium, there are more small independent brewers here than elsewhere in France, but it is also home to Brasserie Sebastien Artois at Armentières, part of the Interbrew Group and France's second largest brewing company.

At right: Kronenbourg is Europe's leading packaged beer. Lutèce recalls that the Romans brewed beer here when the area was known as Lutecia.

At far right: The understated label of St Leonard disguises one of the world's best beers.

At right: The Adelshoffen labels stress the Strasbourg Cathedral and include a wide range of graphic styles, from the traditional to the more modern, for their Alsator low-alcohol beer. Adelshoffen, like Brasserie du Pecheur, is part of the Fischer Group.

At right: Brewing at Hochfelden in the Alsace dates to at least 870. In 1640 Jean Klein built his brewery. It was to remain in his family until 1989, when sold to the Metzger family, relatives of the Haag family Inguiller. In 1927, Louis Haag created the Meteor brand, which is the brewery's flagship label. Others include the premium Ackerland and the newer nonalcoholic beer, Klint.

At right: Brasserie du Pecheur in Schiltigheim brews the flagship brands for the Fischer Group, of which it is a member. These include the premium La Belle Strasbourgeoise. Other products celebrate the fact that the European Parliament meets in Strasbourg. The brewery also markets FischerLei and Panache nonalcoholic beers, and does private label beers for Bennet's and J Sainsbury in England.

At right: Brasserie Sebastien Artois at Armentieres, now part of the Interbrew Group, brews Palten, Platzen, Sernia and Vezelise, as well as producing Interbrew's Belgian products for the French market.

EASTERN EUROPE

Above: **Located in Prague since 1499, U Fleku is the world's oldest brewpub and a mecca for beer lovers from throughout the world.**

Below: **This photo of the brewhouse of the Chernomor Brewery in Odessa was taken before the collapse of the Soviet Union.**

rom the green mountains of Bohemia to the rugged Urals, there lies a great land where beer is known as Pivo (or Piwo) and where the natural evolution of modern brewing was stunted by 45 years of Stalinist tyranny. During that time, the quality of beer declined significantly and labels were little more than merely utilitarian. After the walls came down, many labels remained unchanged, although there are now incentives to improve the quality of the beer.

Czechoslovakia, where brewing has been a part of Czech (particularly Bohemian) culture since the Middle Ages, has always been a notable exception. Despite nearly a half a century of political repression, it continues to rank with Britain, Belgium and Germany as one of the four most important brewing nations in Europe.

There are many important brewing centers in the nation that has been known as Czechoslovakia from 1918 through 1992. Most of them are in Bohemia, including the two largest: Pilsen and Prague (the capital). Located in Prague is the country's largest brewery (pivovary), Staropramen, which was founded in 1869. Prague's other brewery of note is U Fleku, which dates from 1499 and is the world's oldest brew pub. The dis-

tinctive beer brewed at this mecca for brew connoisseurs is found here, and nowhere else in the world. It is not bottled, and as such, has no label.

Pilsen has the distinction of being one of the three corners of the Golden Triangle (the others being Munich and Vienna) where large-scale lager brewing sprang up in the early nineteenth century. The city even gives its name to the lightest, palest of lagers, which are known around the world as pilsner, pilsener or simply pils.

While there are many pilsners, there is only one original Pilsen. This is the beer, first brewed in 1842, that is known in Czech as Plzenky Prazdroj, but known around the world by the words on the distinctive white and gold label: Pilsner Urquell.

The originator of Pilsner Urquell was Martin Kopecky, who supported the idea of developing an outstanding beer that could replace many non-resident beers in Pilsen pubs. Production started on 5 October 1832, and the first barrels were shipped to Pilsen restaurants, but several buckets were sent to publican Karel Knobloch in Liliova Street in Prague, the first man in the kingdom's capital to taste Pilsner Urquell. Its success in the Bohemian spa towns guaranteed that it would eventually be distributed worldwide, in spite of the fact that Prague was a domain of homemade, and frequently renowned, beers. By 1856, the beer from Pilsen was being served in Vienna, and three years later it had reached Paris. The path to the world had begun.

Pilsner Urquell became established in European cities, from Lvov to London and received medals and honors from international shows and exhibitions. Beginning on 1 October 1900, the Pilsen 'beer train' left early every morning for Vienna. A similar train also went to Bremen. By 1874, this Czech beer had arrived in America.

Its trademark, ingenious by its explicitness, was registered in 1898 in a document that referred to the absurdity and illogic of using the word 'Pilsner' for beer brewed in towns outside of Pilsner. The document considered the brewery as inspiring the Urquell in the Pilsner beer, but today the term has become generic.

The Pilsen brewery reached an annual production of over 800,000 barrels (one million hectoliters) before World War I, a number that would not be exceeded for many decades. However, between 1919 and 1923, the the aftermath of the First World War caused uncommonly difficult times for Czech industry.

The domestic market was reduced and many markets abroad were lost. Brewery production gradually subsided proportionally to decreasing marketing possibilities, and an increasing lack of raw materials and manpower. In the late 1930s, production rebounded, and the Pilsner breweries accounted for 75 to 85 percent of the the entire beer export from the country.

Production levels fell again during World War II, and the Communist government seized the brewery after the war. By 1956, however, Pilsner Urquell was once again being exported, bringing in much-needed hard currency for the brewery's new masters. Successive plant modernizations between 1965 and 1985 prepared the original Pilsner for the inevitable market expansion that followed the collapse of Communism in 1989. This event also opened the door to the potential of a wider range of Czech beers reaching Western markets.

Hungary, Bulgaria, Poland and the constituent republics of the former Yugoslavia have indigenous brewing industries, and these products are also starting to appear in the West. In October 1991, the Belgian-based Interbrew Group acquired the Borsodi Sorgyar brewery in Bocs, Hungary.

The former Soviet Union was one of the world's largest brewing nations, ranking fifth behind the United States, Germany, Britain and Japan. Russia still is a major producer but the transition to a market economy has necessitated some fundamental changes, as has been the case in all industries there. For nationally-controlled factories, the breweries of the old USSR had a surprising level of brand identification. While most USSR breweries had such inspired names as State Brewery (PBZ) No 136, others–notably in Lithuania, Latvia and Estonia, as well as Russia–dated to the days before the 1917 Revolution and many actually had colorful labels that suggested a distinction between 'brands.'

Above: This building on Prague's Wenceslaus Square displays the logos of two of the Czech Republic's premier brands: Budvar (Budweiser) of Ceske Budejovice and Prazdroj (Pilsner Urquell) of Pilsen. Adolphus Busch of Anheuser-Busch of selected the beers of Ceske Budejovice (then known as Budweis) as the model for the American national brand he introduced in 1876. Both Budweisers still exist, but not in the same markets.

Below: Brewed in Pilsen (Plzen) and enjoyed around the world, Pilsner Urquell is known domestically as Plzenky Prazdroj.

At right: The Czech city of Ceske Budejovice was known in German as Budweis during the days of the Austro Hungarian Empire in the late nineteenth century. The beer of the city's major brewery was–and still is–known as Budweiser abroad and Budvar at home.

At right: Domestic as well as export labels for Pilsen beer. The most widely known Czech beer in the international market is Pilsner Urquell (known as Plzenky Prazdroj at home). Founded in 1842, the brewery is the nation's second largest brewing company.

At right: Dating from 1869, the Staropramen Brewery in the Capital city of Prague is the Czech Republic's largest.

At right: This selection of Czech labels from the Communist era feature a cornucopia of interesting, if dated, graphics. Golden Pheasant *(third row rom bottom)* is contemporary.

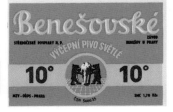

At right: The Warsaw Brewery's main plant and headquarters are situated in the center of Poland's capital city on Grzybowska Street. The company was established in 1848 and has operated continuously at the same location with a malt mill, bottling line and three retail shops in Warsaw and breweries in Kutno, Wyszkow and Ciechanow.

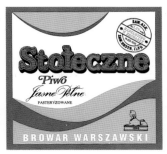

At right: Domestic and export labels from Poland.

At right: Domestic and export labels from Poland and Yugoslavia.

At right: The Aldaris Brewery in Riga, Latvia, dates from 1865. These labels from beer (alus) brewed in the late 1980s celebrated both the city of Riga and the nation's proximity to the Baltic.

At right: Russian labels from the Communist era had a variety of colors, but were graphically similar.

At right: These labels from the Chernomor Brewery in Odessa were in use in the late 1980s, but probably had been designed much earlier.

SOUTHERN EUROPE

Below: The Moretti label's famous painting of the man with the mustache is based on a photograph taken in a cafe in 1942 by Manazzi Moretti. The image is now familiar throughout Italy, Europe and much of the world.

The sun-washed lands of the Mediterranean coast are well-known wine-growing regions. Italy, which the ancient Greeks called Oenotria (the land of wine) produces more wine than France. Spain, Portugal and Greece are also major producers and consumers of wine, with Spain having more acres of vineyards than either France or Italy. In Portugal, 15 percent of the population is involved in the wine industry.

With this in mind, how can there be room for beer? In fact, beer is taking away market share—albeit a tiny sliver—from wine, especially in the cities where beer drinking is developing a cachet among younger drinkers that reminds one of the brasserie scene in Paris.

A large share of the beer market in southern Europe—as can be seen by the signs and labels visible in the cafes and at the beaches—is owned by Heineken and the German brands. These brands are not only imported, but in some cases are brewed in southern Europe. Heineken, for example, owns breweries in Italy, Spain and Greece. There are also several important homegrown brewing companies in the region. The largest brewer in southern Europe is Peroni in Rome, followed by SA Damm in Barcelona, Heineken-owned Dreher in Milan and Heineken-owned El Aguila in Madrid, with Uniao Cervejeira in Portugal close behind. Another prominent smaller brewery—especially in the export market—is Moretti in Udine, Italy, near the Austrian border. Moretti is most noted for its La Rossa, a distinctive dark red beer similar to Peroni's Red Ribbon.

Southern Europe's largest brewer was founded in Vigevano in 1846 by Francesco Peroni. In 1867, Giovanni Peroni transferred the company to Rome. In 1907, the company acquired the ice-making plant near Porta Pia and formed the 'Societa Birra Peroni–Ice and Cold Storage.' In 1924, Peroni built a new plant in Bari and in 1929 took over Birrerie Meridionali Southern Breweries in Naples.

The growth of the Peroni Company continued with its takeovers of the Dormisch Brewery in the northern Italian town of Udine, the Itala Pilsen Brewery of Padova, the Raffo Brewery in Taranto, as well as the Faramia Brewery in Savigliano. In the 1960s, Peroni opened three new, state-of-the-art breweries in Bari, Rome and Padova. In 1988, the company acquired Wuhrer.

Today Birra Peroni Industriale plants are located throughout Italy, from San Cipriano Po, near Pavia, to Bari in the south, from Rome to Naples, from Padova to Battipaglia. With 21 bottling plants that are amongst the most efficient in Europe and 750 tanks capable of handling up to 62 million liters, Birra Peroni produces and markets more than a billion bottles and cans annually. If all these were laid in line, they would stretch for about 80,000 km, circling twice around the globe. The company also produces more than 1.8 million barrels (2.1 million hectoliters) of draft beer.

At far right: SA El Aguila was formed in 1900 and became part of Heineken in 1984. Beers include Aguila (Eagle) Pilsener, and Aguila Master amber lager. Adlerbräu (Eagle Brew) follows the tradition of giving German names to locally produced lagers.

At right: Augusto R Damm founded his Barcelona brewery in 1876, having learned his trade in the Alsace. The Damm family later joined with other brewers, such as Juan Musolas and E Cammany y Cia. From this union, the present SA Damm group was born. Its breweries are in Barcelona, Sta Coloma de Gramenet and El Prat de Liobregat, with the Maltery in Bell-Lloc. SA Damm maintains an active presence in social, cultural and sports events, acting, for instance, as a sponsoring partner in the 1992 Barcelona Olympic Games.

At right: Luigi Moretti founded his brewery in Udine in 1859 when that part of Italy was still annexed to the Austro-Hungarian Empire. In 1989, a large stake in Moretti was acquired by Labatt, Canada's second largest brewer.

At right: Peroni's product line includes the premium Nastro Azzuro, the dark malt Black and the 'rossa' Red Ribbon, as well as Raffo and Wührer products. Wührer was acquired by Peroni in 1988.

At right: Other Italian brands include Pinz Bräu in Crespellano, which, like Moretti, is part of the Labatt Group. Wührer is now owned by Peroni.

AFRICA AND THE MIDDLE EAST

It was here, in Egypt and Mesopotamia, that the art of brewing was first practiced on a large scale more than 5000 years ago. One of the oldest Egyptian brewing recipes comes down to us in a translation by Zosimus of Panopolis, a chemist writing before the time of Photios:

'Take fine, clean barley and moisten it for one day and draw it off, or also lay it up in a windless place until morning and again wet it six hours. Cast it into a smaller perforated vessel and wet it and dry it until it shall become shredded, and when this is so, shake it in the sunlight until it falls apart ... Next, grind it and make it into loaves, adding leaven just likebread, and cook it rather raw, and whenever [the loaves] rise, dissolve sweetened water and strain through a strainer or light sieve ... In baking the loaves, cast them into a vat with water and boil it a little in order that it may not froth nor become lukewarm, and draw up and strain it, and, having prepared it, heat and examine it.' Over the years that followed, indigenous beer styles evolved throughout sub-Saharan Africa that used maize and other plants native to the area. This led to the evolution of beer that was quite different than that which evolved in Europe. In the nineteenth century, as colonialism encroached upon the peoples of what was then known as the 'dark continent,' mass-produced European beer was introduced. Imported beer was quickly augmented by the construction of European-style breweries in Africa itself, notably in Nigeria, Kenya, South Africa and the Belgian Congo. With the power of the industrial revolution's technology behind them, the European brewers were able to effect a major change in the tastes of the African people, and the traditional, native beers all but disappeared.

In 1658, Jan van Riebeeck looked into the possibility of brewing beer in the Cape of Good Hope country near present-day Cape Town. Because yeast and hops had to be imported, his first beer was not of a very high quality. The first professional brewer arrived at the Cape in 1694, and a site for a brewery was approved on Simon van der Stel's farm in Newlands, because, as he said, it had 'the finest and best water available for this purpose.' Today there is a modern brewery at Newlands, still using water drawn from the same natural springs.

Brewing remained a cottage industry for more than two centuries until 1820 when Jacob Letterstedt established Mariendahl Brewery at Newlands. By 1860, this brewery had 60 competitors, mainly Cloetes and Martienssens. When Germans landed in Natal in 1848, there was an increased demand for Cape beer. When the British garrison arrived in Natal, two rival breweries opened in Durban—Crowders Brewery and William Peel's Umlaas Brewery.

In 1862, Anders Ohlsson arrived from Norway and bought the Mariendahl Brewery upon the death of Jacob Letterstedt. In 1883, Ohlsson built Anneberg Brewery. By 1889, he had either absorbed or eliminated much of his competition. Ohlsson's Cape Breweries, Ltd, producing Lion Beer, virtually controlled the Cape brewing industry. Meanwhile, aided by George Raw, Frederick Mead raised the necessary capital and bought William Peel's Umlass Brewery in Durban, which was the birth of a Natal brewery syndicate.

With the gold rush in the Transvaal came a

Below: **The people who built the pyramids at Giza quenched their thirst with a beverage called** *hekt* **(beer). The Egyptians had a highly developed brewing industry at least 5000 years ago, and some authorities theorize that ancient people domesticated grain to brew beer before they domesticated grain to bake bread.**

beer rush. Charles Chandler set up the first Transvaal brewery, Union Breweries, in 1887 in Ophirton. His most noteworthy competitor was the Castle Brewery, founded by Charles Glass. In 1887, Frederick Mead arranged to purchase Glass's Castle Brewery, and this resulted in the formation of South African United Breweries, Ltd. Mead knew that growth was essential, and a large, new building was erected in Johannesburg. The market growth from this brewery was tremendous, and with the injection of investments, a new company, the South African Breweries, Ltd (SAB) was formed on 15 May 1895.

In 1899, SAB entered the Cape market by purchasing the Martienssen Brewery in Cape Town. By this time, the Castle label had been adopted for all SAB beers, and soon this brand began to make inroads into Ohlsson's territory. With his Lion brand having lost ground in the Cape, Ohlsson diverted his attention to the Witwatersrand and bought the Thomas Brewery. Soon sales exceeded the capacity of this brewery and the Lion Brewery was built at Braamfontein in 1906. Up until now, the market had been in Johannesburg, Durban and Cape Town, but now SAB expanded to Bloemfontein, Port Elizabeth and Salisbury, Rhodesia (now Harare in what is now Zimbabwe).

Because of its size, SAB and its Castle brand had no real fear of opposition. They made their first of many moves toward a merger with Ohlsson's Cape Breweries, but Anders Ohlsson rejected it. Before World War II, both SAB and Ohlsson went through a prosperous period, reaching an agreement which regulated the relations between the two companies in the hotel and bar trade. Despite the serious shortages in raw materials, both of them survived the war and the great depression that followed.

However, telling blows came in the form of excise duty, which made beer the most heavily taxed beverage on the market. Because of this, beer prices increased, which led to a measurable decrease in consumption, and as a result, Ohlsson's Cape Breweries and Union Breweries merged into SAB in 1956. Today SAB is the leading brewing company on the African continent, with a near-total market share in the southern part of the continent. This includes all the above brands, as well as license-brewed Heineken and Amstel.

During the nineteenth century, German and British breweries were opened in Egypt and the Middle East, just as the French were developing the sunny hills of Morocco, Algeria and Tunisia for viticulture. As with the European lands on the north side of the Mediterranean, beer drinking was never too widespread in this region, except among British and German expatriates, who were numerous until the mid-twentieth century and the rise of nationalism. Sine the 1970s, with the resurgence of fundamentalist Islam–which forbids the consumption of alcohol–many of the breweries that had thrived in the region, particularly those in Iran, have closed. Notable breweries in the area today include Efes in Turkey, Al Chark in Syria, National in Israel and the Jordan Brewery in Amman, Jordan.

When the Jordan Brewery Company, Ltd was founded in 1955 by Sa'd Abujaber & Sons, a Jordanian group and Amstel Brewery (now part of the Heineken group) of Amsterdam. The company built a brewery at Zerka north of Amman. Malt and maize are still regularly imported from Holland, Belgium and France, and Styrian hops were imported from Yugoslavia until 1976 when the brewery began using hop concentrate imported from Germany. The first Jordan Amstel Beer was distributed to the market in October 1958, and in 1964, this beer was awarded the Gold Medal in Paris. In 1972, the company began draft beer sales in designated outlets. In 1987, there was a merger with the General Investment Company, Ltd, and in September 1989 the company bought Arab Breweries Company, Ltd.

Below: **A group of young South Africans pause for a few beers, in this case, a few Castle Lagers from South African Breweries. SAB adopted Castle as its primary brand name early in the twentieth century.**

At right: The combine that includes Arab Breweries and Jordan Breweries in Amman produces Petra and Vita, as well as Amstel and Henninger under license.

At right: The labels of South African United Breweries, Ltd include the famous independent brand names that merged to form SAB in 1956, including Ohlsson's Cape Breweries, Ohlsson's Lion Brand and that of the old Castle Brewery. With roots that go back to seventeenth century Cape Town, SAB is now headquartered in Johannesburg.

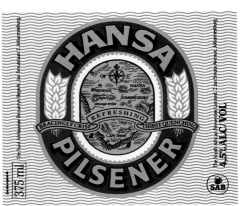

At right: The SCBK Brewery at Pointe Noire near Brazzaville in the Republic of the Congo exports a beer known as Ngok', the phonetic spelling of *Le Choc,* which means 'crocodile.' The Ngok' was the symbol of the pre-colonial Ki-Kongo region of equatorial Africa. The beer is a lager rather than a pre-colonial style.

Also at right: Solibra brews Mamba, an export lager, at its brewery at Abidjan, capital of the Ivory Republic.

Above: In addition to their Gold de Star brand, Brasseries Star in Madagascar produces Three Horses Pilsener and Guinness under license.

Above: Located on the island of Mauritius, the brewery of the same name produces Phoenix Lager Beer, a Pilsener type. Brewed since the beginning of Mauritius Breweries operations in 1963, Phoenix won the Gold Medal at Brewex in 1983 and the Gold Medal at Monde Selection in 1989.

Stella Lager Beer, brewed since 1964, won a Gold Medal at Brewex in 1976 and at the Monde Selection in 1981 and 1989. Blue Marlin Lager Beer has been brewed and bottled since 1989 and won a Gold Medal at the Monde Selection in 1992.

ASIA AND THE PACIFIC

Above: In the Philippines, the familiar San Miguel label is not really a label at all, but rather white enamel serigraphed and baked onto the glass.

Opposite page: Today the Archipelago Brewery Company (ABC), makers of Anchor Beer, are owned by Asia Pacific Breweries (APB) of Singapore. This Anchor Beer is not to be confused with the products of the Anchor Brewing Company of San Francisco, California or the other breweries of the same name in England, Belgium and elsewhere. For some reason, the anchor has always been a popular emblem for brewers.

The earth's largest continent, with 60 percent of its population, produces less beer in real terms and less beer per capita than any other continent, except Africa. The major exceptions are Japan–the world's fourth largest brewing nation–and China, which between them produces 75 percent of the beer brewed in Asia.

After Japan and China, South Korea and the Philippines are roughly tied for a distant third place.

In Asia, as in Africa, there are local copies of European-style lagers produced in most countries, and there are still many indigenous native beers to be found in the more remote corners of the continent.

Like so many other elements of Western culture, beer was introduced into Japan by Commodore Matthew Perry when he made his historic visit in 1853.

There were some subsequent local attempts to brew domestic beer in Japan, but the first successful commercial brewery was set up in 1869 at Yokohama by the American firm of Wiegand & Copeland.

This brewery, later sold to Japanese interests, evolved into the Kirin Brewery Company, Ltd, which is today the largest brewing company in the Far East and the fourth largest in the world after Anheuser-Busch and Miller in the United States and Heineken of the Netherlands. Kirin currently maintains brewing facilities in Amagasaki (Osaka), Fukuoka, Hiroshima, Kyoto, Nagoya, Okayama, Sendai, Shiga, Takasaki, Gochigi, Tokyo, Toride and Yokohama. Kirin exports to Europe and Asia, but Kirin beer for the North American market is brewed in Canada.

Kirin labels used in the United States say 'imported' but the beer is imported from Canada, not Japan.

Sapporo Breweries, Ltd was founded in 1876 in the northern city of the same name that is seen as the mecca of Japanese brewing culture. Because Kirin brews in Canada, Sapporo is the leading Japanese import in the North American beer market, a fact of which the company enjoys reminding consumers. As with other Japanese brewing companies, Sapporo is deeply involved in real estate and leisure time activities, as well as in producing other beverages, including soft drink and wines made with grapes from its own vineyards.

Suntory was founded in 1899 by Shinjiro Torii, a vintner intending to develop a wine for export. In 1923, he built the first whiskey distillery in Japan at Yamazaki near Kyoto, thus founding the Japanese whiskey industry.

Beer was not added to the product line until 1963. Today Suntory is really more of a vastly diversified real estate/leisure services company than a beverage producer. Nevertheless, Suntory, along with Asahi, complete the list of Japan's top four brewing companies.

As in Japan, brewing in China had its origins in the nineteenth century with the arrival of Westerners.

The Germans built a brewery at Tsingtao (now Qingdao) and the beer which is brewed there–Tsingtao Lager–still bears the most widely recognized label of any beer exported from China.

In the Philippines, the largest and best known brand and brewing company was also the first brewing company in the Southeast Asia.

Don Enrique Barretto de Ycaza founded his La Fabrica de Cerveza de San Miguel in 1890, eight years before the Spanish relinquished control of the Philippines to the United States in the Spanish-American War.

Korea's largest brewing company is the Oriental Brewery Company, Ltd in Seoul, which markets OB Lager.

In Singapore, Asia Pacific Breweries (APB) produces a line of beers and stouts–led by Tiger Beer–that have received many international accolades and awards.

Formerly known as Malayan Breweries, Ltd (MBL), the company was formed in 1930 as a joint venture between the Fraser & Neave Group of Companies (F&N) and Heineken NV of Holland.

In 1946, writer Anthony Burgess, while searching for a title for his book about life in Malaysia and Singapore, obtained permission to use the then advertising slogan for APB's Tiger Beer, 'Time for a Tiger.'

At right: Part dragon and part horse, the 'Kirin' on Kirin's labels is a symbol of happiness that was first 'seen' by the mother of Confucius. This graphic depiction of the creature has remained unchanged for the better part of a century.

At right: Sapporo's product line includes lagers, and a 'black' beer. Named for a good luck deity, Yesibu was first introduced in 1887. Sapporo describes this highly regarded beer as a 'stout draft,' although it is technically neither.

At right: Labels from throughout Asia include some of the various nations' most recognized export brands: Thailand's Singha, Korea's OB, China's Tsingtao, Hong Kong's Sun Lik and San Miguel from the Philippines and Hong Kong.

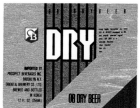

At right: Suntory was founded as a winery in 1899 and began distilling whiskey in 1923, but didn't start to brew beer until 1963.

At right: These Indian labels include the products of the Kalyani Breweries (Calcutta), the Mohan Nagar Brewery (Uttar Pradesh) and the Solan Brewery (Mimachal Pradesh). Mohan Meakin, Ltd, which owns Mohan Nagar, was founded in 1855. Taj Mahal is a popular export brand, while Golden Eagle is the largest selling brand in India.

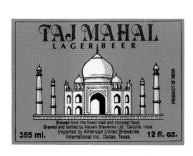

At right: Singapore's Asia Pacific (originally Malayan Breweries) began brewing Tiger lager in 1930 and now also brews Archipelago Brewery's ABC Extra Stout and Anchor Pilsener.

AUSTRALIA AND NEW ZEALAND

ustralia and New Zealand, despite small populations, have robust brewing industries, with brewers whose roots extend back to the eighteenth century. The two largest Australian brewing companies are Carlton & United Breweries (CUB), whose flagship brand is the ubiquitous Foster's Lager, and the Bond Group, which owns numerous brands, including Swan Lager out of Perth and Tooheys, with breweries in New South Wales. The Bond Group also bought Heileman's in the United States, which until 1990 made it one of the world's largest brewery holding companies. The most widely recognized ale brand is Cooper's of Leabrook in the state of South Australia.

In New Zealand, the largest brewing company is the Lion Corporation, which also does business as New Zealand Breweries, Ltd and whose flagship brand, Steinlager, is well known in the export market.

Beer first arrived in Australia with the early ships from Britain in 1788. A free settler, John Boston, made the first commercial beer in Australia in 1796 from malted maize and Cape gooseberries. He and his successors not only had to cope with the hot climate and poor quality ingredients, but also with the problem that the beer deterio-

rated when it was transported long distances by ox carts to be sold.

While the most common type of beer in Australia today is lager, it did not make an impact on local production until the 1880s. Before that, ales were made–and in most cases, not very well. The hot weather encouraged beer drinking, but it also played havoc with yeast. 'Tasteless, insipid and sugary' was the verdict on locally made beer in the early days of colonial settlement. It was the larger breweries, specifically Tooheys and Tooths in New South Wales, who in the 1870s sorted out the quality problems by using select ingredients and cleaning up the entire lager-making process.

Matthew and Honora Toohey emigrated from Ireland in 1841, and settled in rural Victoria to raise cattle, but they moved to Melbourne in 1860 to take up the license of the Limerick Arms Hotel in Emerald Hill. In 1865, on a visit to Sydney, their son John Thomas Toohey heard that the Darling Brewery was for sale and convinced his brother James Matthew to join him in the business. Trading as JT and J Toohey, their company prospered, and after a few years they expanded to a larger site.

Tooheys and the rival Tooth & Company rose to dominance in the 1880s with the

Above: **The leading export brands from down under include Foster's from Australia and Steinlager from New Zealand.**

Right: **An important part of the early brewing process was barrel making (coopering). From 1875, a pale blue band between two of the hoops, was the registered trademark for Tooheys and an easy way to ensure that the workers did not mix up barrels. This photograph dates to the 1920s and shows a racking line at the old Standard Brewery site in Sydney.**

Facing page: **An artfully posed bottle of Tooheys Red with the distinctive Stag label** *(see caption on page 88).*

Above: **These Tooheys labels date from the early twentieth century. The stag symbol can be traced to John Toohey's favorite hotel, the Bald Faced Stag Hotel in Leichhardt. Though not used on all products, the stag symbol has been part of the history of Tooheys since 1869.**

Top right: **The Cascade Brewery in Tasmania was built in 1824, with top stories added in 1927.**

popularity of their beers. They remained rivals for a century. Their differences included religion–the Tooheys were Catholic while the Tooth family in England were Anglican. It was Tooths, however, which dominated the market in New South Wales for most of the time by supplying their beer to a massive hotel network 'tied' to the brewery. Changes in the liquor industry from the mid-1950s helped Tooheys break this monopoly. The emergence of clubs and liquor shops allowed Tooheys to respond to the developments, while Tooths retained their focus on hotels. However, Tooheys position was not sustained, and the revitalization of the old Tooth Brewery under the guidance of Carlton & United Breweries saw the latter wrest the laurels back from a struggling Tooheys in the 1980s.

Eventually, Tooheys merged with the Queensland brewer Castlemaine Perkins in March 1980, and ownership of Tooheys shifted to the Bond Corporation in September 1985, and then to National Brewing Holdings in October 1990.

Now part of the Elders IXL Group, Carlton & United Brewers have their roots in the old Carlton Brewery, born during the golden age of brewing in the 1850s at a time when the city of Melbourne had 35 breweries. Today CUB is a holding company that spans

more than a century and a half and includes 126 breweries. The flagship brand, Foster's, is ironically named for a pair of American brothers who spent only about 18 months in Australia. They founded their Foster Brewing Company in Melbourne in 1887, sold it the following year and went home, never to be heard from again.

When CUB was formed as a multi-company consortium in 1907, Carlton was the largest partner, followed by McCracken's, Victoria and Castlemaine, with Shamrock and Foster's being the two smallest components. Foster's quickly grew in importance within CUB, and by 1937 posters were already declaring it 'Australia's National Beverage.' Fifty years later, Australian film personality Paul Hogan, a Foster's spokesman, declared that 'Foster's is Australian for "beer," mate!'

Western Australia, far from the more populous Melbourne/Sydney areas, got its first brewery–James Stokes' Albion Brewery–in Perth in 1837. The Swan Brewery, which was to become the brewer of Australia's second most identifiable lager brand, was built by Frederick Sherwood in Perth in 1857. Captain John Maxwell Ferguson and William Mumme of the Stanley Brewing Company, leased the Swan Brewery in 1874, and around 1887acquired the Lion Brewery.

In 1908, the name of the Stanley Brewery was changed to Emu Brewery, and in 1928, Swan purchased Emu. In 1978, Swan moved from Perth to a large, modern new brewery constructed at Canning Vale, Western Australia, and in 1982, Swan became a wholly owned subsidiary of Bond Corporation Holdings, Ltd.

In 1985, Bond purchased Castlemaine Tooheys, Ltd, and by 1987, The Swan Brewery Company, Tooheys and Castlemaine Perkins, together with the Pittsburgh Brewing Company of Pennsylvania and G Heileman Brewing Company of Wisconsin, made up the Bond Brewing Group of Companies. However, in 1990, Swan, together with Tooheys and Castlemaine Perkins, were purchased by National Brewing Holdings, a joint venture partnership between Bell Resources, (now Australian Consolidated Investments) and Lion Nathan. The Swan Brewery Company became a wholly owned subsidiary of Lion Nathan Australia in 1992.

In Tasmania, the island state off the tip of Victoria, the Cascade Brewery Company, Ltd was incorporated in 1883. A cordial and aerated water plant was installed in 1885 to meet the demands of a growing population for soft drinks, and in 1922 the company acquired J Boag & Son, brewers of Boag's beer at Launceston. In 1923, the company entered the wine and spirit trade, and for a time, the grocery business, by the acquisition of Traders Pty. In 1981, Industrial Equity, Ltd (IEL) succeeded in gaining more than 50

percent of Cascade and purchased the remaining shares in 1985. Following the share market crash of October 1987, IEL sold Cascade to Wilson Neil Australia and the name was changed to the Cascade Group in 1988.

The export market is important to the brewing companies down under because of the small population, but nevertheless, both Australia and New Zealand have proven to be fertile grounds for American-style brewpubs since the early 1980s. The first of these was Terry McCashin's Roc Mac Brewery, which opened in Stoke, New Zealand in 1982.

Above: **The Shire Horses used by Swan are one of the oldest and longest breed of heavy horses in the world. Horses like those pictured here, have provided the traditional means of beer deliveries throughout the world. Swan Teamsters, Steve Lockhart and Liz Pronk, drive the team, look after the horses, dray and harness.**

Below: **Compare this contemporary view of the Swan keg line to that of the Tooheys coopers shown on page 86.**

At right and in the second row: Acquiring the heritage of 126 breweries, the brands of the Carlton & United Breweries include Foster's, as well as Abbot's, Abbotsford, Ballarat Bitter, Brisbane Bitter, Cairns' Carlton, KB, NG, Melbourne Bitter, Victoria Bitter and Sheaf Stout. Fiji Bitter is brewed by a Carlton brewery in Fiji.

 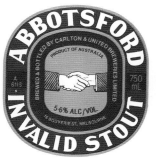 

At right: For the birds: The Swan product line includes those of the sign of the graceful swan, as well as those of the flightless Emu, a bird native to Australia. Swan traces its history to 1856 and Emu to 1837, although the Emu name dates from 1908. Swan purchased Emu in 1928, but the later retained the brand name identification.

  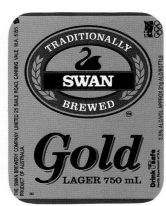

At right: When John and James Toohey's brewery was incorporated at the turn of the century, the stag became the trademark. When the company moved to Auburn, the cornerstone of the building was a bas relief of a sitting stag.

At right: In Tasmania, Cascade uses a variety of illustrations, including its distinctive brewery building on its labels. J Boag & Son of Launceston was acquired in 1922 and the separate brand identification was retained. Razor Edge was developed for the American market with a label featuring fauna more common to northern Australia than Tasmania.

At right: Cooper's Brewery, founded in 1862 in South Australia, is Australia's leading brewer of top-fermented beers which include Pale Ale and Stout. Cooper's also brews Oakbank Ale and license brews Birell (of Switzerland) nonalcoholic beer and Swan Stout.

LATIN AMERICA AND THE CARIBBEAN

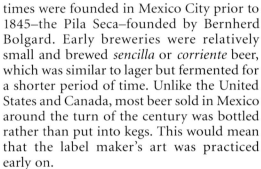

Latin American brewing began with the Indians and then with the first Spanish brewery, or *cervecería*, established in the 1500s. In the ensuing three centuries, however, Latin American tastes paralleled those of Spain, just as North American tastes paralleled those of England, and this meant an inclination toward wine and distilled spirits, such as mescal and tequila rather than beer *(cerveza)*. There was also *pulque*, a fermented beverage favored in the nineteenth century by peasants. Even through an influx of German immigrants in the mid-nineteenth century, the tropical nature of much of Latin America prevented the brewing of lager until the latter part of the century when artificial ice-making technology became widely available.

The first Mexican breweries of modern times were founded in Mexico City prior to 1845–the Pila Seca–founded by Bernherd Bolgard. Early breweries were relatively small and brewed *sencilla* or *corriente* beer, which was similar to lager but fermented for a shorter period of time. Unlike the United States and Canada, most beer sold in Mexico around the turn of the century was bottled rather than put into kegs. This would mean that the label maker's art was practiced early on.

Though brewing in Mexico did not develop as quickly as it did in the United States and Canada, it has made great strides since the 1970s, when Mexico surpassed Canada as a brewing nation. Like Canada, Mexico's current brewing scene is overwhelmingly dominated by a 'big three,' of which two have merged to leave a 'big two.' Cuauhtemoc, Moctezuma and Modelo all developed from breweries established in the late nineteenth century by German or Swiss immigrants.

In September 1985, Cuauhtemoc and Moctezuma joined under the umbrella of Valores Industriales, becoming the largest brewing company in Mexico and fifteenth largest in the world. Both partners continue, however, as separate operating groups, and are listed below in their pre-merger configurations. They have separate foreign distribution, but share a common distribution network within Mexico.

By the 1970s, many of Mexico's brands were available as imports in the United States. Indeed, the largest growth by any imported brands in the American market has been among Mexican beers.

In 1986 alone, Moctezuma's Tecate enjoyed a 28 percent increase in popularity, while Modelo's Corona increased its share by an incredible *169 percent*, an unprecedented increase that made it second only to Heineken among imported beers in the United States market.

Brazil is the second largest brewing nation in the Western hemisphere, a third again larger than third place Mexico, and with about a fifth of the production of the United States. The other major South American brewing nations are Columbia and Peru. Chile, a major wine producer, does not rank as one of the continent's major

Below: Corona Extra, Modelo's flagship lager, uses an enamelled 'label' serigraphed onto the face of the bottle. Brewed in Mexico for years and exported to the United States for nearly as long, Modelo achieved a monumental increase in market share in the late 1980s. It passed a half dozen competitors to become the second biggest import after Heineken in the American market.

brewing nations. With much of Mexico's production being exported to the United States, the largest single *brand* of beer sold in all of Latin America is Brahma, which is brewed in Rio de Janeiro, Brazil by Cervejaria Brahma.

Most beer brewed in South America–as in the rest of the world outside of England and Ireland–is lager.

However, there was an indigenous native 'black' beer brewed here in pre-Columbian times, which is still brewed in remote corners of the Upper Amazon.

The purest form of this unique native-style brew that is available in the outside world is Xingu *(shin-gu)*, named for a tributary of the Amazon River. The beer was 'discovered' and nurtured for export by Alan Eames, the noted beer anthropologist. It is now brewed in export quantities at Cacador, Brazil, by Cervejaria Cacador.

The total beer production of Central America is less than six million barrels (6 million hectoliters), but the area has a long brewing tradition.

The Mayan-speaking peoples of pre-Columbian (before 1492) Central America favored a beer made by fermenting cornstalks, while the Uto-Aztecans and others (such as the Pueblo and Tarahumar) of northern Mexico and the border country brewed a sprouted maize beer. Known as *Tesguino* or *Tiswin*, this beer was produced in a manner that is more reminiscent of familiar brewing processes.

For the tribes, such as the Maya, of the Yucatan peninsula, corn and corn products were the central focus of their lifestyle, from food to religion.

Today however, the tradition has shown more direct influence from German-trained brewers in the latter twentieth century than any of the nations to the north. German-style lagers and pilsens are much more common than in Mexico, owing to the region's more tropical climate.

The brewing tradition of the little golden flecks which are the islands of Caribbean is long and varied. In the beginning it was the aboriginal people and their *tesguino* beer and then the English with their imported beers. By the seventeenth century, when brewing was really taking hold on the mainland to the north, the isles of the West Indies had already gone over en masse to the warm embrace of rum.

By the nineteenth century there was the enigmatic Guinness West Indies Porter that may have been brewed there, perhaps in Barbados or possibly Jamaica. It may even have been brewed in the British Isles and brought to the Keys at high tide by wily traders who pretended that it was the local brew. No lager could be brewed there because there was no

ice, but then English tastes tended to give lager a wide berth in any event, and it was English tastes that formed the tastes of West Indian beer drinkers.

By 1898, there were just seven breweries in the entire region: one each in Barbados, Trinidad and Cuba, and four in Jamaica.

When the United States defeated Spain in the Spanish-American War, Obermeyer & Liebmann came south from Brooklyn to open a second brewery in Cuba's capital. Today there are still eight, but the faces of the players have changed.

In Jamaica, Desnoes & Geddes has been brewing Red Stripe (which had originally been ale but was reformulated as a lager in 1934) for 60 years. Red Stripe was the Caribbean's best known brand elsewhere on the continent.

Holland's giant brewer, Heineken, the largest in Europe, licensed its products to Desnoes & Geddes, and it owns breweries in the Antilles and Trinidad.

From Denmark, Carlsberg is licensed in the Dominican Republic and Guinness is brewed in Jamaica.

Above: **The Carta Blanca and Tecate labels are prominent on this Cerverama in Jalisco, Mexico.**

At right: Cervecería Cuauhtemoc, named for the Aztec emperor who died in 1521 and headquartered in Monterrey, Nuevo Leon was Mexico's second largest brewer prior to its being joined with Moctezuma under the Valores holding company. The company's flagship brand is Carta Blanca, but another important brand is Tecate.

At right: Cervecería Moctezuma, headquartered in Mexico City, was established in 1894 at Orizaba, Veracruz by Adolph Borkhardt, Henry Manthey, Wilhelm Haase and C von Alten. In 1985 Moctezuma, along with Cuauhtemoc, became part of Valores Industriales. Moctezuma's flagship brands are Dos Equis (XX) and Superior. Other brands include Tres Equis (XXX), Sol, Noche Buena and Bavaria.

At right: Cervecería Hondurena evolved through mergers in the years 1915 to 1965. These companies individually marketed the Salva Vida (1916) brand in La Ceiba, the Imperial (1930) and Nacional (1953) brands in Teguciagalpa, and the Ulva (1928) brand in San Pedro Sula. The products of the brewery include Port Royal Export.

At right: Caribbean labels from Banks (Barbados), Brew Master's (San Juan, Puerto Rico), India (Mayaquez, Puerto Rico), Medalla (Puerto Rico), Bohemia (Dominican Republic), Nacional Dominicana (Dominican Republic) and Constancia (El Salvador).

At right: Beer labels from Bolivia, Brazil, Columbia and Peru. Though they're both Brazilian, a lager like Brahma represents a style vastly different from a black beer like Xingu. In Peru, Callao brews both a Pilsen-style lager and a rare, dark beer that is similar to Xingu.

At right: Cervecería Modelo, head-quartered in Mexico City, DF is Mexico's largest single brewing company. Modelo's well-known Corona brand *(see page 92),* which has been brewed in Mexico for decades and exported to the United States for years, became a phenomenal 'overnight' success in 1986 in the American market.

At right: Desnoes & Geddes of Kingston, Jamaica was founded in 1918 as a soft drink business by Eugene Desnoes and Thomas Geddes. It is today managed by their heirs, with Peter Desnoes as the most recent past chairman and Paul Geddes as the current chairman. Red Stripe Lager and Dragon Stout are the flagship brands.

THE UNITED STATES

Above: **These vintage US labels from the collection of Charles Finkel bring back memories of a bygone era. Many icons are here, such as the eagle and the German and Bohemian names that are still used to imply style or origin.**

Facing page: **St Louis is home to the flagship brewery of Anheuser-Busch, the world's largest brewing company.**

The history of brewing in the United States began with the Indians of Mexico and the American Southwest, but most of our present traditions arrived with the European immigrants. The English brought their top-fermenting ale yeasts with them and immediately established breweries in the Colonies. By the time of the American Revolution, ales and porters were well developed as part of daily life, and most landowners were as likely to have a brewhouse on their grounds as a stable. Among America's early statesmen, not only Samuel Adams, but both George Washington and Thomas Jefferson were brewers.

In 1840, the first wave of German immigrants introduced bottom-fermenting yeasts to American brewing, and United States soon became a land of lager drinkers. By the end of the nineteenth century there were 4000 breweries located in nearly every small town and city neighborhood, each with its own special style of beer. The idea of a town or neighborhood brewer was no more unusual than a town baker or neighborhood butcher.

By the turn of the century, the advent of a continental railroad network and invention of artificial ice making made possible the rise of megabrewers like Schlitz, Pabst and Anheuser-Busch, who became large, regional brewers, and by World War II were in a position to launch truly national brands. With the rise of the national brands, small local and regional brewers suffered, and many disappeared as nearly everyone attempted to create pale lagers that would appeal to as wide an audience as possible.

Today the United States is the world's biggest brewing nation, with an annual output of over 180 million barrels (214 million hectoliters), double that of second-place Germany and triple that of third-place Great Britain. The largest American brewing *companies* by market share are Anheuser-Busch (42 percent), Miller (22 percent), Coors (10 percent), Stroh/Schlitz (10 percent), and Heileman (8 percent). The leading *brands* by market share are Anheuser-Busch's Budweiser (28 percent), Miller Lite (11 percent), Bud Light (6 percent) and Coors Light (5 percent).

Anheuser-Busch of St Louis is not only the largest brewer in the United States, but the largest brewer in the world, with no close rivals. The company brews 80 million barrels (100 million hectoliters) of beer annually. The world's biggest brewing company traces its roots to a small brewery started in St Louis, Missouri in 1852 by Georg Schneider and taken over in 1860 by Eberhard Anheuser. Four years later Anheuser's son-in-law Adolphus Busch (1839-1913) joined the firm. A marketing genius, Busch turned the small city brewery into a national giant. He launched the extraordinarily successful Budweiser brand as a mass-market beer in 1876, and in 1896 he introduced the Michelob brand as the company's premium beer. Originally a draft beer, Michelob was not marketed as a bottled beer until 1961.

Today Anheuser-Busch's flagship brewery is still located in St Louis, but beginning in 1951 eleven other breweries were established from coast to coast.

Miller Brewing of Milwaukee has been the second largest brewing company in the United States since the late 1970s after a long climb from eleventh place in 1965. The brewery originated in suburban Milwaukee, Wisconsin in 1855 as Charles Best's Plank Road Brewery. It was purchased in 1855 by Frederic Miller, who turned it into one of the region's leading breweries. In 1969 the Philip Morris Tobacco Company acquired 53 percent of Miller Brewing, and the following year they bought the remaining 47 percent. Miller produces over 40 million barrels (48 million hectoliters) annually and operates six plants located at Albany, Georgia; Eden, North Carolina; Irwindale, California; Fort Worth, Texas; Fulton, New York; and Milwaukee, Wisconsin. The Milwaukee brewery is the largest, producing 8.5 million barrels (10.1 million hectoliters) annually, but the Eden and Albany plants are close behind with an annual production rate of eight million barrels (9.5 million hectoliters) each.

Miller's flagship brand is Miller High Life, a premium national lager brand that has existed since before Prohibition. In 1975, Miller introduced Lite, the first nationally marketed reduced-calorie beer. It went on to become the leading reduced-calorie beer, as

well as the second best selling beer of any kind, in the United States. (Budweiser is first.) An important Miller product since 1975 is Löwenbräu, produced under license from the brewer of the same name in Munich, West Germany, where it has been produced since 1893. (In Canada, Molson brews Löwenbräu.) While Miller brews a German beer in the United States, Miller High Life is brewed in Canada by Carling-O'Keefe and in Japan by Sapporo.

The Adolph Coors Company of Golden, Colorado operated for 114 years at the same site high in the Rocky Mountains that was selected by Adolph Coors himself in 1873. Coors has grown from one of scores of tiny, regional breweries that once dotted the nation's landscape, to the third largest brewing company in the United States. At the same time, its brewing plant in Golden is the single largest brewery in the world, with an annual output of 18 million barrels (21.4 million hectoliters). In 1987, Coors celebrated the grand opening of its second brewery in Virginia's Shenandoah Valley, near the town of

Elkton, a plant with a 2.5 million-barrel (3 million-hectoliter) capacity.

Stroh Brewery of Detroit became the fourth largest brewing company in the United States in May 1982 when it purchased the much larger, but financially ailing, Joseph Schlitz Brewing Company. Schlitz, whose brand name Stroh retained, had been one of the two largest brewers in the United States since the nineteenth century. Despite its being in fourth place after the Schlitz acquisition, Stroh's market share declined through most of the mid-1980s. Started in 1850 by Bernhard Stroh, the company survived Prohibition but remained a regional brewery until well after World War II. The acquisition of Schaefer in 1981 and of Schlitz the following year catapulted Stroh from seventh to fourth place among United States brewers.

The G Heileman Brewing Company of La Crosse, Wisconsin is a unique example of a small regional brewer that grew to national prominence, not through the vehicle of a single national brand like Anheuser-Busch

Below: **The big copper brewing kettles at the 18-million barrel Coors brewery in Golden, Colorado. Until very recently the Golden facility was the largest single brewing plant in the entire world. This is indicative of the massive scale of brewing and beer consumption in the United States.**

or Miller, but through an amazing amalgam of important, formerly independent, regional brands. Established in La Crosse by Gottlieb Heileman and John Gund in 1858, Heileman remained a small regional brewer until the early 1960s, when it began to acquire other smaller regional breweries, such as the acquisition of Associated Breweries in 1963 and Blatz in 1969. Other major regional brands acquired by Heileman include Oregon's Blitz-Weinhard, Seattle's Rainier, Minnesota's Grain Belt and Lone Star, the so-called 'national beer of Texas.' In 1987, Heileman was acquired by Alan Bond of Australia, whose holdings constituted one of the world's largest multinational companies, and included brewers of Swan Lager. Pittsburgh Brewing Company–brewers of Iron City Beer– was acquired by Bond in 1986 and integrated into the Heileman regional network to further strengthen Bond's North American brewing operation. The Heileman acquisition made Bond Brewing the sixth largest in the world.

Pabst Brewing Company of Milwaukee, Wisconsin was the largest brewery in the United States at the turn of the century and has remained in the top six ever since. The original brewery was started in 1844 by Jacob Best and later run by Philip Best in partnership with Captain Frederick Pabst. The Captain essentially ran the brewery himself after Philip retired in 1866. Pabst acquired Olympia Brewing in 1983 (which had recently acquired Theodore Hamm's brewery in St Paul, Minnesota) and was itself taken over in February 1985 by the reclusive California millionaire Paul Kalmanovitz, who already owned Falstaff, General and Pearl.

Since the beginning of the 1980s, the brewing industry in the United States has been enjoying a renaissance. After four decades of decline in the number of brewers, over one hundred microbreweries and brewpubs have opened their doors.

Inspired by Fritz Maytag's extraordinary success with San Francisco's Anchor Brewing, the microbrewery revolution began in California but soon spread across the nation. Among the important early pioneers were Sierra Nevada Brewing in California (1980), Boulder Brewing in Colorado (1980), Mendocino Brewing in California (1982), Yakima Brewing in Washington (1982), Buffalo Bill's in California (1983) and Widmer Brewing in Oregon (1984). Mike McMenamin of Portland, Oregon opened his first brewpub in 1985 and now owns a chain of over a dozen. Meanwhile, on the east coast in 1985, Jim Koch had his recipe for Samuel Adams lager produced under contract, and an extensive market for his beer was well established by the time that he actually began brewing in Boston in 1987.

Compared to what was available as late as 1980, the spectrum of beer styles being brewed on this continent today is nothing short of incredible. Not only is there the best selection of lagers in over half a century, but Americans are able to choose from ales and wheat beers, and brewers are producing distinctive stouts and have even helped to revive the art of porter brewing, which had all but died out even in England. American brewers are also developing more esoteric beer styles. Best of all, the United States now has fresh local brands again as in the nineteenth century.

Top: **Brewer and beer importer Charles Finkel in the brewhouse of his Pike Place microbrewery in Seattle.**

Above: **Two Kentucky blondes: Oldenberg Brewery's Kelly Craven with a pallet of Oldenberg Blonde. Founded in 1987, Oldenberg was the first microbrewery in Kentucky. Today it boasts the largest beer hall in North America.**

Left: **The Miller brewery in Milwaukee is today the largest such facility in the city whose name was once synonymous with the American industry.**

At right: Abita Brewing was founded in the town of Abita Springs, Louisiana in 1986.

Also at right: Alaskan Brewing & Bottling (formerly Chinook Alaskan) is located in the town of Douglas, near Juneau, Alaska. Established in 1986, it is the first brewery to be built in Alaska since Prinzbräu folded in 1979.

At right: Alpine Village Hofbräu, a brewpub which opened during 1988 in the city of Torrance, California, is partly owned by the Hofbräuhaus Traunstein in Bavaria.

Also at right: Albuquerque Brewing & Bottling is a brewpub in Albuquerque, New Mexico.

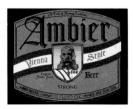

At right: Anchor Brewing Company was originally established in San Francisco in 1896. Appliance heir Fritz Maytag bought the company in 1965 when it was on the verge of collapse and turned it into the very model of an efficient, smaller regional brewery. Over the years Maytag increased the brewery's output from 600 barrels (714 hectoliters) to 45,000 barrels (54,000 hectoliters) annually.

The company's flagship product is Anchor Steam Beer, one of the West's most prized premium beers, which was developed by master brewer Maytag himself, and is loosely based on what is known of the legendary 'steam' beers produced in Gold Rush days. Other Anchor products include Anchor Porter, Anchor Liberty Ale, Old Foghorn Barley Wine-style Ale, which was first produced in 1975. Anchor is renowned locally for its annual Christmas beer, which has been specially brewed since 1975, with a different recipe each year.

At right: Anderson Valley Brewing of Booneville, California operates a brewpub called The Buckhorn Saloon, a successor to the original Buckhorn Saloon that was established in 1873.

At right: In addition to 'Bud' and Michelob, Anheuser-Busch brews a variety of other beers. Busch, introduced in 1955, is marketed regionally east of the Rocky Mountains. In 1988 and 1989, Busch received gold medals in the American Pilsner category at the Great American Beer Festival. In the late 1970s and early 1980s, the company introduced a family of low-calorie or 'light' beers. These included Natural Light (1977), Michelob Light (1978) and Bud Light (1982).

In 1981, Anheuser-Busch introduced Michelob Classic Dark, which has been a consistent award winner at such events as the Great American Beer Festival, where it competes alongside some of the nation's best specialty beers. In 1984, the company not only added a malt liquor called King Cobra to its family of products, but also became the first major brewer to mass market a reduced-alcohol beer, which they call 'LA.'

At right: Aspen Beer Company was founded in 1988 in Aspen, Colorado. Its Aspen Silver City Ale is brewed under contract at Boulder Brewing.

Also at right: Bayern Brewing operates the Northern Pacific Brewpub, an establishment with a Bavarian theme, opened in August 1987 in the former Northern Pacific Railway station in Missoula, Montana.

At right: The Berghoff is an old Chicago restaurant famous for its 100-foot bar and for its private label Berghoff Beer, which is regarded by many as Chicago's 'hometown beer.' It traces its heritage to the brewery started in 1887 in Fort Wayne, Indiana by Herman Josef Berghoff of Dortmund, Germany. Berghoff introduced his beer to the Windy City at the 1893 Chicago World's Fair and opened the restaurant at its present site in 1898. In 1989, Berghoff bought Huber, forming the Berghoff-Huber Brewing Company.

At right: Blue Ridge Brewing, Virginia's first microbrewery, is located in the town of Charlottesville.

At right: Boston Beer Company was founded in 1985 by Boston entrepreneur Jim Koch. Initially, Koch's flagship brand, Samuel Adams Boston Lager, was available only in Boston, Massachusetts and Munich, Germany, but is now in nationwide distribution in the United States. After having had his beer contract brewed by Pittsburgh Brewing for two years, Koch moved production to a renovated 40,000-barrel (48,000-hectoliter) brewery in Boston in 1987. The brewery's other brands include Samuel Adams Double Bock and Boston Lightship.

At right: Boulder Brewing Company of Boulder, Colorado, which began operations in 1980, is the second largest Colorado-based brewer after Coors.

At right: BridgePort Brewing is a brewpub located in the city of Portland, Orgeon.

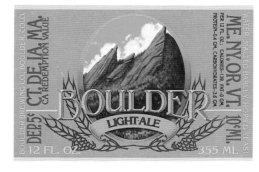

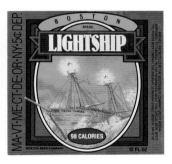

At right: British Brewing was founded in 1988 in Glen Burnie near Baltimore, Maryland by brewmaster Stephen Parkes and his partner Craig Stuart-Paul. Using only imported malts and hops, they have recreated the ales of their homeland, Britain.

Also at right: The Brooklyn Brewery, founded in 1988 by Stephen Hindy and Tom Potter, features Brooklyn Lager. A dry-hopped 'pre-Prohibition' style lager, the beer is actually brewed under contract by FX Matt Brewing in Utica, New York.

At right: Buffalo Bill's of Hayward, California became one of the first three brewpubs to open in the United States since Prohibition when brewmaster Bill Owens opened for business in September 1983. In 1988, Owens opened a second brewpub, Bison Brewing Company, in nearby Berkeley, California, which has since been sold.

At right: Capital Brewery is a micro-brewery opened in June 1986 in the town of Middleton, Wisconsin.

At right: Catamount Brewing of White River Junction, Vermont, which produced its first beer in 1987, was the first commercial brewery to operate in Vermont since 1893. Initial distribution included only Vermont and New Hampshire, but has been expanded to other New England states since 1988.

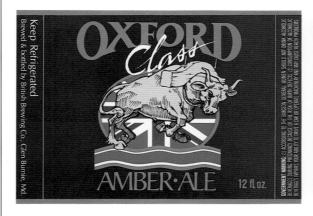

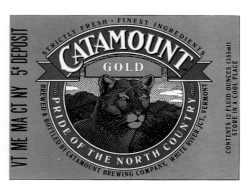

At right: Clark's USA was established by Lyman Clark in 1985 in Washington, DC. Clark's is the only beer produced in the United States that has *no* alcohol.

Also at right: Founded in May 1988 in Cleveland, Ohio, Cleveland Brewing's only brand is Erin Brew. The lager is brewed under contract by Pittsburgh Brewing.

At right: Cold Spring Brewing of Cold Spring, Minnesota dates back to the brewery started by George Sargel in 1874 and evolved to its present name by 1898.

At right: Commonwealth Brewing is located in Boston, Massachusetts.

At right: The Coors product line is headed by the flagship Coors Banquet brand, the complementary low-calorie Coors Light (which is known as the 'Silver Bullet' because of the natural aluminum finish of its can), and a seasonal beer called Winterfest.

Other products include the distinctively colored George Killian's Irish Red, an ale brewed under license from the original Irish brewer, and three premium beers introduced in the 1980s called Herman Joseph's, HJ Light and Coors Extra Gold Draft.

At right: Dead Cat Alley is a brewpub located, appropriately, on Dead Cat Alley in Woodland, California. Master brewer Jim Schlueter began bottling Dead Cat Lager, Cat Tail Ale and Fat Cat Porter in August 1989.

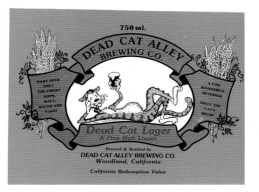

At right: Devil Mountain Brewery is a brewpub located in Walnut Creek, California.

Also at right: Dixie Brewing of New Orleans was established in 1907 and was, until recently, the only remaining brewery in the Louisiana city that once was the brewing capital of the entire South.

At right: Dock Street Brewing was founded in 1986 by Philadelphia chef Jeffrey Ware.

Also at right: Dubuque Star Brewing in Dubuque, Iowa was established as Star Brewing in 1898 and took the name of its hometown in 1904.

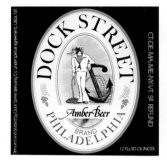

At right: Falstaff Brewing of Fort Wayne, Indiana traces its roots to the Forest Park Brewing Company of St Louis, Missouri that was established in 1910 and taken over by 'Papa Joe' Griesdieck in 1917. Renamed Falstaff (after the Shakespeare character) during Prohibition, the company expanded to become one of the Midwest's strongest multisite regional brewers. Today, the Ballantine and Narragansett brands, once major labels in the northeast, are part of the Falstaff group.

At right: General Brewing Company of Rochester, New York is the seventh largest brewer in the United States. The company traces it heritage back to the brewery established in 1855 by Jacob Rau. This business evolved into the Genesee Brewing Company in 1878. In February 1985, Genesee bought the Fred Koch Brewery of Dunkirk, New York.

At right: DL Geary Brewing was founded in 1988 in Portland, Maine. Brewing of Geary's Pale Ale is under the direction of brewmaster David Geary.

At right: Golden Pacific Brewing is a microbrewery begun in 1985 in Emeryville, California. In 1989, Golden Pacific signed an agreement with Thousand Oaks Brewing to begin producing their products in Emeryville.

At right: Hales Ales, Ltd is a micro-brewery located in Colville, north of Spokane, Washington that was established in 1984.

At right: Hart Brewing Company of Kalama, Washington, north of Vancouver, is one of the many microbreweries that sprang up in the Pacific Northwest during 1984 and 1985.

At right: Heileman's original brand and largest seller is Old Style. Also in the line are the complementary Old Style Light and the premium Heileman's Special Export.

Others of the mainly regional brands include: Iron City (Pittsburgh Brewing), Lone Star—the 'national beer' of Texas, Rainier in Seattle and the Blitz Weinhard brands from Portland, Oregon, notably Henry Weinhard's Private Reserve.

At right: Hibernia Brewing of Eau Claire, Wisconsin began in 1878 as Henry Sommermeyer's Dells Brewery. Later the brewery was known as John Walter's City Brewery and then Walter Brewing. In 1985 it was purchased by Michael Healy, and it became Hibernia Brewing, after the Latin name for Ireland.

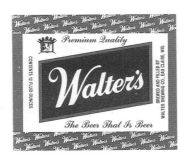

At right: Hood River Brewing and its adjacent White Cap Pub opened in 1987 in the town of Hood River, Oregon. Full Sail won a gold medal at the 1989 Great American Beer Festival.

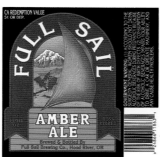

At right: Joseph Huber Brewing of Monroe, Wisconsin evolved from the Bissinger Brewery established in 1845. Between 1848 and 1906, it operated successively under the names John Knipschilt, Ed Ruegger, Jacob Hefty, Fred Hefty and Adam Blumer. It survived as Blumer Brewing until 1947, when it became Joseph Huber Brewing. In 1985, when Paul Kalmanovitz took over Pabst, the latter's president and vice president purchased Huber. In 1989, Huber was in turn purchased by the Berghoff in Chicago, a restaurant for whom it had long brewed a house brand beer. The resulting company is now known officially as Berghoff-Huber Brewing.

At right: Hudepohl-Schoenling of Cincinnati, Ohio, known locally as 'Cincinnati's Brewery,' was created in December 1986 by the merger of Hudepohl Brewing and Schoenling Brewing. Hudepohl originated with Gottfried Koehler in 1852 and was taken over as the Buckeye Brewery of Ludwig 'Louis' Hudepohl and George Kotte in 1885. The company became Hudepohl Brewing in 1899. In 1982, the company introduced Christian Moerlin, a superpremium brand named for one of Cincinnati's first great brewers, whose famous brewery was started on Elm Street in 1853 but did not survive Prohibition. Schoenling Brewing was established in 1934 on the heels of the repeal of Prohibition.

At right: Humboldt Brewery is a brewpub located in the town of Arcata on California's north coast.

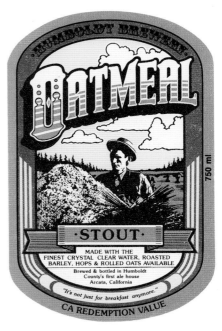

At right: Jones Brewing of Smithton, Pennsylvania was established by Welsh immigrant William B 'Stoney' Jones in 1907 as the Eureka Brewing Company, but because Stoney habitually made personal sales calls to taverns in the area, it came to be known as 'Stoney's Beer.'

At right: Kemper Brewing on Bainbridge Island in Washington's Puget Sound is a microbrewery founded in 1984.

At right: Latrobe Brewing of Latrobe, Pennsylvania was established in 1893 at a time when the town's only other brewery was located at St Vincent's Abbey and operated by Benedictine monks. The flagship brand is named for the nearby Rolling Rock Estate, a horse ranch. An intriguing detail about Rolling Rock is the presence of the mysterious '33' symbol that appears on the back of the bottle. The company itself cannot remember why it was put there in the first place because the product was introduced in 1939. Among the most popular answers to the riddle are that Prohibition was repealed in 1933; there are 33 words on the back of the 12 ounce Rolling Rock bottle; or that there are 33 letters in the ingredients list—water, malt, rice, corn, hops, brewer's yeast.

At right: Jacob Leinenkugel Brewing of Chippewa Falls, Wisconsin was built in 1867. Located on top of Big Eddy Springs, the brewery was known as the Spring Brewery until 1898. In 1987, the company was purchased by Miller Brewing of Milwaukee, but it remains autonomous as a separate operating unit. Every label carries the Indian maiden head ('Leinie') motif. This reflects the brewery's location in 'Indian Head Country,' so named because of the Indian profile created on maps by the meanderings of the Mississippi River along the Wisconsin-Minnesota border.

At right: The Lion, Incorporated, also known as Gibbons Brewery, of Wilkes-Barre, Pennsylvania was founded in 1905 as the Luzerne County Brewing Company and became Lion Brewing in 1910. It has used the Gibbons, Stegmaier and Pocono brand names.

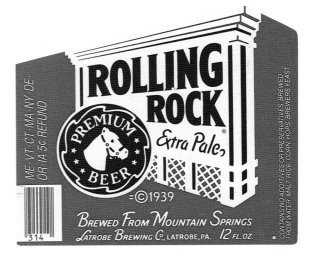

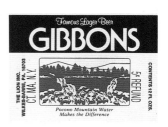

At right: Long Island Brewing contracts the production of Montauk Light, with FX Matt Brewing in Utica, New York. Maine Coast Brewing in Portland, Maine also contracts with FX Matt.

At right: Mad River Brewing Company was founded by veteran brewmaster Bob Smith in 1989. Mad River is noted for Steelhead Extra Pale Ale.

At right: Manhattan Brewing of New York City was known for its horse-drawn beer wagons.

Third row: Marin Brewing Company of Larkspur (Marin County), California was founded in April 1989 by Brendan Moylan.

Third row: Massachusetts Bay Brewing, a microbrewery which calls itself simply Mass Bay Brewing, is located in Boston with distribution throughout New England.

Far right: FX Matt Brewing of Utica, New York (also known as West End Brewing) evolved from the Columbia Brewery established by Charles Bierbauer in 1853. The company was taken over in 1888 by Francis Xavier Matt I (grandfather of the current president, FX Matt II) and organized as West End Brewing. The brewery was renamed for FX Matt in 1980. The brand name Utica Club, introduced for the soft drinks produced by the company during Prohibition, was retained afterward for West End's beer products.

At right: Mike McMenamin of Portland, Oregon and his brother Brian operate more than a dozen restaurants and pubs in western Oregon. Among them are six brewpubs, making the McMenamin group the largest *chain* of brewpubs in the United States. The first was the Hillsdale Brewery. Opened in Portland in October 1985, it was the first to be established in Oregon since Prohibition. The other McMenamin sites are the Cornelius Pass Roadhouse & Brewery at Hillsboro; the Fulton Pub & Brewery in Portland; The Thompson House Brewpub in Salem; the Highland Pub & Brewery at Gresham; the High Street Brewery & Cafe in Eugene; and the Lighthouse Brewpub overlooking the Pacific Ocean at Lincoln City.

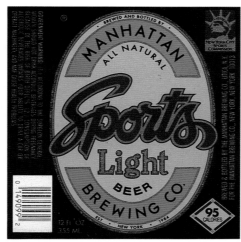

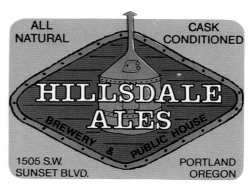

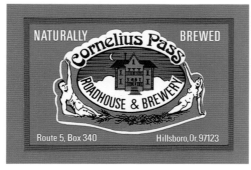
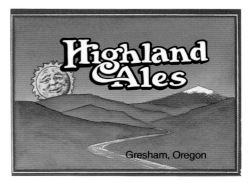

At right: Mendocino Brewing in Hopland, California was founded by Michael Laybourn, Norman Franks and John Scahill in 1982. It was California's first brewpub since Prohibition and produces about 8000 barrels (9500 hectoliters) a year. Its brands are typically named for birds of the region and include Black Hawk Stout, Blue Heron Pale Ale, Eye of the Hawk, Peregrine Pale Ale and Red Tail Ale.

At right: Miller Brewing began in Milwaukee, Wisconsin in 1855 as Charles Best's Plank Road Brewery. Purchased the same year by Frederic Miller, it became one of the region's leading breweries. In 1969 and 1970 the Philip Morris Tobacco Company bought Miller Brewing, beginning its long climb from the eleventh largest brewing company in the United States to the second largest.

The company's flagship brand is Miller High Life, a premium national lager that has existed since before Prohibition. One of the most successful brands produced is Miller Genuine Draft, a nonpasteurized draft-style beer.

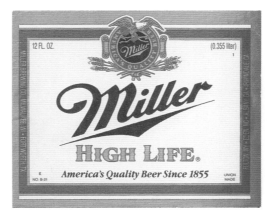 

At right: Millstream Brewing of Amana, Iowa was founded by Joe Pickett, Sr, with the first bottling in December 1985.

At right: Monterey Brewing is a microbrewery and brewpub located on Cannery Row in Monterey, California.

Also at right: Napa Valley Brewing of Calistoga, California also operates the historic 1882 Calistoga Inn, a brewpub, restaurant and hotel. A brewery located in the heart of North America's premier wine-producing region may seem to be out of place, but Napa Valley Brewing's beers are just as world class as the wines being produced from the adjacent fields.

 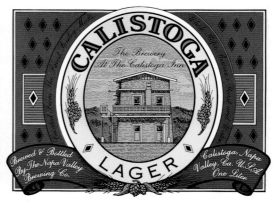

At right: Montana Beverages of Helena, Montana was established in 1982 by Dick Burke and Bruce De-Rosier to brew beer under the Kessler brand name. It was first produced in 1984 and is a reference to the original Kessler brewery, which was started in 1865 by Luxembourg native Nick Kessler and later grew into one of Montana's most important breweries.

By 1957, the market for small breweries in Montana, as in most of the rest of the United States, had been reduced to the point where it was no longer economically viable. Kessler Brewing closed, and its copper kettles were shipped to South America.

When Montana Beverages revived the Kessler brand 27 years later, it was an entirely new beer and an entirely new market. Today under the direction of master brewer Julius Hummer, the brewery produces the Kessler brand beers, as well as brewing under contract for companies in Eugene, Oregon, Santa Barbara, California and Jackson Hole, Wyoming.

At right: North Coast Brewing was founded in Fort Bragg on California's Mendocino County coast in 1988, and produces Red Seal Ale, Scrimshaw Pilsner Style Beer and Old No 45 Stout, as well as seasonal brews.

At right: Old Marlborough Brewing of Marlborough, Massachusetts was founded in 1989 by Larry Bastien and three partners: Joseph Cunningham, AJ Morgan and Barry McCarthy. Their Post Road Real Ale–named for the old New York to Boston thoroughfare–is produced under contract by Catamount Brewing in White River Junction, Vermont.

At right: Old New York Beer Company is headquartered on Washington Street in New York City but its El Paso and Baja, two Mexican-style premium beers, are brewed under contract by FX Matt Brewing in Utica, New York.

At right: Founded in Boston by amateur brewer Rick Dugas, Olde Time Brewers began brewing its popular Ironside Ale in 1992.

Also at right: The Oldenberg Brewery of Fort Mitchell, Kentucky, near Cincinnati, is complemented by a complex that includes a vast beer hall, beer garden and a restaurant. With the Western Hemispshere's largest collection of brewing memorabilia, Oldenberg is also home to the American Museum of Brewing History & Arts.

At right: The major Pabst brand is Pabst Blue Ribbon, one of the oldest name brands in American history. Other Pabst-owned brands include Hamm's. The Pabst-owned Olympia Brewery at Tumwater brews Olympia (aka 'Oly').

At right: James Page Brewery is a microbrewery founded in 1987 in Minneapolis, Minnesota.

Facing page: Pike Place Brewery is a microbrewery which opened in the historic Pike Place Market in Seattle, Washington in October 1989. It is owned jointly by internationally known beer importer Charles Finkel and brewmaster John Farias, who oversees the brewing of Pike Place Pale Ale and other specialty beers.

At right: Pearl Brewing of San Antonio, Texas developed out of a brewery started in 1881. The company became Pearl Brewing in 1952, although the brand name had been used since 1886 by San Antonio Brewing. Having become associated with General Brewing in 1978, Pearl became part of the group of breweries assembled by Paul Kalmanovitz prior to his death in 1987.

At right: Red Hook Ale Brewery of Seattle, Washington was established by Paul Shipman in 1982 in the city's Ballard district. Brands include Red Hook Ale, Black Hook Porter, Ballard Bitter and Winterhook Christmas Ale.

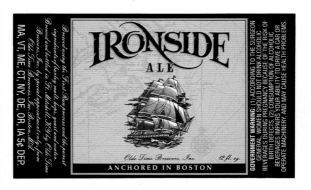

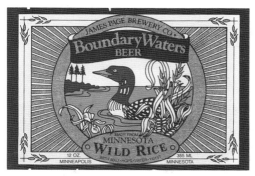

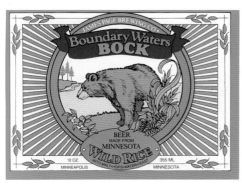

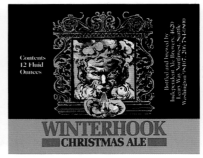

At right: Reinheitsgebot Brewing produces its Collin County beers in Plano, Texas.

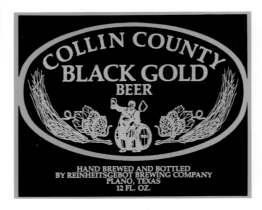

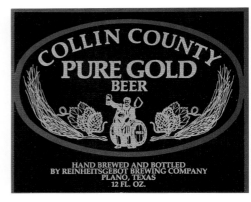

At right: Santa Cruz Brewing brews bottled beer for the local, northern California market and operates the Front Street Pub in Santa Cruz, California. The principal brands brewed here are Lighthouse Amber, Lighthouse Lager and Pacific Porter.

At right: San Francisco Brewing is located on the site of the historic Albatross Saloon on Columbus Avenue in San Francisco. America's fourth brewpub, brewing began here in 1986 under the direction of owner and master brewer Allen Paul.

At right: Santa Fe Brewing was founded by Mike Levis in June 1987 in Gallisteo, New Mexico. The only brand is Santa Fe Pale Ale.

At right: August Schell Brewing of New Ulm, Minnesota was established in 1860. The brewery survived the 1862 Sioux uprising because of August Schell's good relations with the Indians, and has existed as a small regional brewery ever since.

At right: Schirf Brewing, located in the Wasatch Mountains at Park City, Utah, is the only brewery to operate in Utah since 1967. Founded as a microbrewery in October 1986, Schirf expanded into its Wasatch brewpub in July 1989.

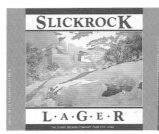

At right: Sierra Nevada Brewing of Chico, California was founded in 1980 by Paul Camus and Ken Grossman as one of the nation's first microbreweries. Sierra Nevada is one of the largest microbreweries in the United States.

At right: Spoetzl Brewery of Shiner, Texas dates from 1909. In 1989, the company was purchased by Gambrinus Imports, the San Antonio-based importer of Modelo's Corona brand.

Third row: Sprecher Brewing is a microbrewery located in Milwaukee, Wisconsin with brewing under the direction of master brewer Randy Sprecher.

At far right: Stanislaus Brewing of Modesto, California was established by Garith Helm, who began commercial production in 1984. The 'patron saint' of Stanislaus Brewing is 'St Stan,' a public relations man who assumes the character of Brother Stanislaus, who is said to have brewed for Frederick the Great a beer inspired by divine intervention. Stanislaus produces only altbier, that German-style, top-fermented brew similar to ale.

At right: Stevens Point Brewery of Stevens Point, Wisconsin dates from 1857. The success of the Stevens Point Brewery and its Point Special Beer was traditionally seen as being due, at least in part, to its decision to limit distribution to a very narrow geographical area, permitting demand to exceed supply.

At right: Carol Stoudt's Brewing Company serves a brewpub called Stoudt's Black Angus in Adamstown, Pennsylvania.

Also at right: Straub Brewery in St Mary's, Pennsylvania was started by Captain Charles Volk in 1872 as an extension of his City Hotel, and was taken over by Peter Straub, Volk's former brewmaster, in 1876. Thereafter, except for two years (1911-1913) as the Benzinger Spring Brewery, the brewery has carried the Straub name.

At right two rows: The Stroh Brewery Company's own brand name products are complemented by Erlanger Premium Beer, Signature Super Premium, Schaefer, Piel's, and of course Schlitz.

Schlitz was one of the most recognized brand names in the United States from the time it was first marketed by Joseph Schlitz in 1858 until 1982, when the company, having fallen on hard times, was acquired by Stroh.

Milwaukee was once the capital of American brewing and they used to say that 'Schlitz was *the* beer that made Milwaukee famous.'

At right: Summit Brewing is a microbrewery located in St Paul, Minnesota. The principal brands brewed here are Extra Pale Ale, the award-winning Great Northern Porter, Sparkling Ale and Christmas Ale.

At right: Sun Valley Brewing is a microbrewery located in the town of Wood River, Idaho near the Sun Valley ski resort. The brewery has been in operation since November 1986, and the principal brands brewed here are Our Holiday Ale, Sawtooth Gold Lager, White Cloud Ale and Yule Ale.

At right: Telluride Beer Company of Telluride, Colorado markets Telluride Beer and Telluride Winter Ale. These are produced under contract by Berghoff-Huber.

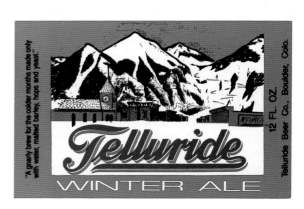

At right: Vernon Valley Bräuhaus is a microbrewery located in Vernon, New Jersey.

Also at right: Winchester Brewing is a brewpub which opened in San Jose, California in July 1988 and began selling packaged beer in December 1989.

At right: Yakima Brewing & Malting is a microbrewery established in 1982 in Yakima, Washington in the heart of North America's greatest hop-growing region. Under the direction of founder Herbert Grant, the brewery produces beer for both the retail market and for Grant's own brewpub.

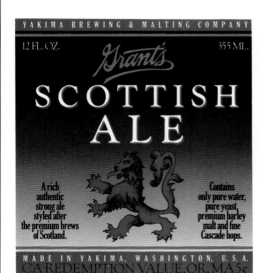

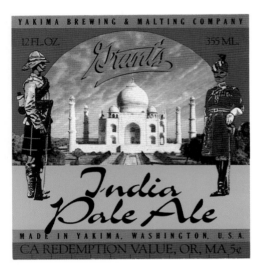

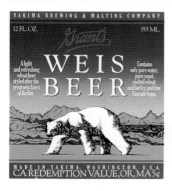

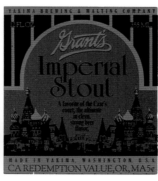

At right: Yuengling & Son was established in 1829 by David G Yuengling. It stands as the oldest brewery in the United States and, after Molson in Canada (1786), as the second oldest in North America.

Today the 200,000-barrel (238,000-hectoliter) brewery is still family owned and operated under president Richard Yuengling.

CANADA

As the United States was beginning to grapple with forming its identity as a nation, life continued as before in that vast tract of land to the north called British North America, and which one day would be called Canada.

Early home brewing had followed similar patterns as in the more densely populated United States, but the first big name in Canadian brewing was John Molson. From the English county of Lincolnshire, Molson arrived in Montreal in 1782 armed with a copy of John Richardson's *Theoretical Hints on the Improved Practice of Brewing*.

The people of Quebec, predominantly French, preferred wine, so there was little of a brewing tradition in this province. Since imported English beer sold for more than rum in Montreal, the city's beer drinkers welcomed John Molson's first brewery, which began brewing in 1786. Today Molson Breweries (Brasserie Molson in Quebec) is the oldest brewing company in all of North America. The headquarters and the flagship three-million-barrel (3.6-million-hectoliter) brewery are located in Montreal, and

the company's other breweries are located in Barrie, Ontario, Vancouver, British Columbia; Edmonton, Alberta; Winnipeg, Manitoba; Prince Albert, Saskatchewan; Regina, Saskatchewan; and St John's, Newfoundland. The Sick's Lethbridge Brewery in Lethbridge, Alberta has been a Molson subsidiary since 1958.

Long the second biggest brewing nation in North America, Canada yielded that distinction to Mexico in the mid-1970s. Of the big three, Labatt's is Canada's number one brewer and Molson traditionally has had the largest Canadian share of the lucrative export market to the United States. In 1989, however, Molson and Carling O'Keefe announced their intention to merge into a single entity to be called Molson Breweries. This new entity would then become Canada's premier brewer, with better than half the market. (For the sake of clarity, Carling O'Keefe and Molson are considered here in their premerger configurations.)

Carling O'Keefe, Ltd (Brasserie O'Keefe L'tee in Quebec) was the result of the nineteenth century merger of the breweries of Sir

Above: Vintage nineteenth-century labels from John Labatt's original London, Ontario brewery.

Right: **Throughout the twentieth century, Labatt's flagship pilsener has been referred to colloquially as 'Labatt's Blue' because of its label, but the company has only used the actual phrase on the label in recent decades. When the low-calorie version of the flagship product came on line in the 1970s, there was no doubt as to what it would be called. Another important product is Labatt's 50, an anniversary ale.**

Facing page: **Molson's huge plant overlooking the river in Montreal is on the site of John Molson's first brewery which he built here in 1786.**

Above: John Labatt's Pilsener 'Blue' and Light Pilsener 'Blue Light' products.

Right: A stunning array of mainly regional products from Labatt's breweries. Unlike 'Blue' and 'Blue Light,' Labatt does not brew or market these products in all provinces. The names Oland and Alexander Keith are prominent in the Labatt family tree. The Oland family also played a part in the founding of Moosehead.

John Carling (established by his father, Thomas Carling, in 1840) and Eugene O'Keefe (established in 1862). In the 1950s and 1960s, Carling O'Keefe expanded its operations into the United States through its subsidiary company, Carling National Brewing, which once operated 14 breweries in 11 states. In fact, in 1960 Carling National was the fourth largest brewer in the United States. After this high point, the market share of the subsidiary declined, and Carling, like many other brewers, was forced into closing its American plants.

John Labatt, Ltd (Brasserie Labatt L'tee in Quebec) was founded by John Labatt in London, Ontario in 1853 and still maintains the corporate headquarters there, wtih the brewing headquarters for the company in Toronto.

Despite the dominance of the big three, several smaller breweries still exist and new microbreweries have been started in British Columbia and Nova Scotia since the mid-1980s. The big three were, however, the only brewing companies with breweries in more than one province, and as a result, they are the only brewers with national distribution. An interesting aside to the big three is that each had a flagship or most popular brand which was identified by a color. These were Carling O'Keefe's *Black* Label, Labatt's Pilsen *Blue* and Molson *Golden*.

At right: Amstel Brewery Canada, formerly Hamilton Breweries, began operations in 1981 and is now owned entirely by Heineken NV of the Netherlands. Headquartered in Hamilton, Ontario, the products brewed here include Steeler Lager, which is considered Hamilton's 'hometown' beer, and Grizzly, a lager originally brewed only for the United States export market but now available in Ontario as well. A major part of Amstel's operation, of course, is devoted to brewing the parent company's Amstel and Amstel Light brands.

At right: Big Rock Brewery was founded in 1985 by Ed McNally and is located in Calgary, Alberta. Big Rock takes advantage of the fact that Calgary is in the heart of a fertile grain-growing region.

At right: Brick Brewing began operations in Waterloo, Ontario in 1984.

Also at right: Conners Brewing began brewing in 1985 in Don Mills, near Toronto, Ontario.

At right (both rows): Carling O'Keefe's flagship brand is Black Label Beer, which is brewed at all seven Carling O'Keefe breweries across Canada. Other brands in regional distribution include Red Cap Ale, Alta 3.9, Black Horse, Calgary Lager, Carling Pilsner, Champlain, Dominion Ale, Dow Ale, Heidelberg, Kronenbräu 1308, O'Keefe Ale, O'Keefe Extra Old Stock Malt Liquor, O'Keefe Light, Old Vienna, Standard Lager, Trilight and Toby. In addition to its own brands, Carling O'Keefe brews Miller High Life under license from Miller Brewing in the United States and Carlsberg under license from the Carlsberg Breweries of Copenhagen, Denmark.

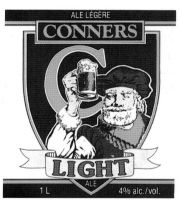

At right: Drummond Brewing is located in Red Deer, Alberta.

At right: Granite Brewery of Halifax Nova Scotia was established in 1985 and was the first Canadian microbrewery and brewpub outside British Columbia.

At right: Labatt's flagship brand, and the leading single brand of beer, is Labatt's Pilsen, which is better known (because of its label) as 'Labatt's Blue.' The company's other brands fall into three categories: other company-owned national brands (like 'Blue' and 'Blue Light'); foreign brands brewed under license by Labatt in Canada; and company-owned regional brands, which may be brewed only in one or two provinces.

The national brands include Labatt's 50 Ale (introduced as a special promotion in 1950), John Labatt Classic, Labatt's Light (Légère) and Labatt Select. The latter two are low-calorie beers introduced in 1978 and 1984, respectively.

Labatt's major regional brands are Kokanee Pilsener Beer, which is popular in British Columbia; Club Beer in Manitoba; Crystal Lager Beer in Ontario; Blue Star in Newfoundland; and Alexander Keith's India Pale Ale, which is the largest selling brand of beer in the Maritimes. Other Labatt's regionals are Cervoise, Columbia Pilsener, Cool Spring, Country Club Stout, Extra Stock Ale, Gold Keg, Grand Prix, IPA (India Pale Ale), Jockey Club Beer, Kootenay Pale Ale, Manitoba 200, Old Scotia Ale, Schooner, Skol, Super Bock, Velvet Cream Porter, Velvet Cream Stout and White Seal Beer.

At right: Molson's flagship brand is Molson Golden, which is a national brand in Canada and the biggest selling Canadian export brew in the United States. Other Molson beers include Molson Light (Légère) and Molson Export Ale. Special regional beers are also brewed by Molson's western breweries (British Columbia, Alberta, Manitoba and Saskatchewan).

At right: Moosehead Breweries of St John, New Brunswick were founded by a family of Anglo-Swedish descent named Oland, who also founded Oland Breweries now owned by Labatt's. Thanks in part to a successful marketing campaign in the early 1980s, Moosehead's products are extremely popular in the United States. They are, in fact, more popular in the United States than they are in Canada.

At right: Northern Breweries, Ltd is headquartered in Sault Sainte Marie, and has breweries in Sudbury, Thunder Bay and Timmins. Thunder Bay brews only Superior Lager and Thunder Bay, and Timmins brews only Northern Ale. The plant in Sudbury brews and bottles Northern and Encore Beer.

Fourth row: Oland Breweries, Ltd of Halifax, Nova Scotia was founded by the same Oland family that started Moosehead. Oland breweries operate in Halifax as Oland Brewery and St John, New Brunswick as Labatt's New Brunswick Brewery. Both breweries produce Labatt's and Oland products, while Halifax brews Keith's India Pale Ale and St John brews Labatt's Light.

Bottom row: Pacific Western Brewing of Prince George, British Columbia was originally established in 1957 under the name Caribou Brewing. Five years later, it was bought by Carling O'Keefe and sold to Ben Ginter and rechristened Tartan Breweries. It was sold again in 1981 to WR Sharpe who operated it as the Old Fort Brewing Company until 1984, when the name was changed to Pacific Western Brewing. In 1989, Pacific Western purchased Simcoe Brewing in Ontario and Granville Island Brewing in Vancouver.

At right: Rocky Mountain Brewing of Red Deer, Alberta (formerly owned by 'Uncle' Ben Ginter and now a subsidiary of Steeplejack Services in Calgary) operates the only independent brewery in the fast-growing, oil-rich province on the eastern side of the Canadian Rockies.

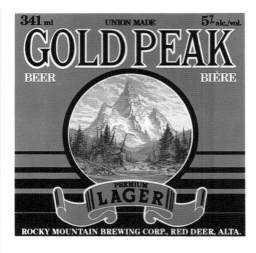

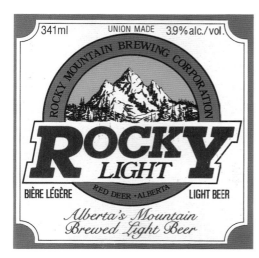

At right: Strathcona Brewing of Edmonton, Alberta is a microbrewery that was founded in 1986.

At right: Upper Canada Brewing was founded by Frank Heaps in Toronto, Ontario in 1985. The principal brands brewed here are Dark Ale, Rebellion Malt Liquor, True Bock and True Light.

INDEX

128

Acknowledgements:
The author would like to gratefully acknowledge all of the breweries' generosity in providing the labels and information for this book. The author would also like to thank Ruth DeJauregui for her help in researching this book. In addition, the following individuals provided invaluable assistance: Roger Stuhlmuller at Acme Food Specialties; Don Shook of Adolph Coors; Dr Jürgen Auckenthaler at Adambräu Gesellschaft; Paul I Nunny at Adnams and Company; Michael Buckner of Albuquerque Brewing; Gill Freshwater at Allied Breweries; Carl Glauner at Alpirsbacher Klosterbräu; Gibbs Mewple at Anchor Brewing; Mark Carpenter and Fritz Maytag of Anchor Brewing; Carl Bolz and George Westin of Anheuser-Busch; Sarah Koh at Asia Pacific Breweries; Jodi A Pilotto at Barton Beers; Robert Peyton of Basso & Associates; Michael Tassin at Belukus Marketing; M Weber at Bières de Chimay; M Breuer and M Wrobel at Binding-Bräuerei; V Moro at Birra Moretti; Michael Meinardus at Bitburger Pils; Paul Summers of Blue Ridge Brewing; Jim Koch of Boston Beer Company; Jean-Pierre Eloir at Brasserie de l'Abbaye Des Rocs; Chris Bauweraerts at Brasserie D'Achouffe; Marie André Cherty at Brasserie Dubuisson Frères; Oliver Debus, Valentine Brau and Roger Knauss at Brasserie Fischer; François Entz at Brasserie Meteor; Gunter Graefenhain at Brau & Brunnen USA; Kristine Deicke at Bräuerei Aying; Caroline Schaller at Bräuerei zum Gurten; Marie Peacock of Brick Brewing; Robin Hinz of BridgePort Brewing; Stephen Hindy of the Brooklyn Brewery; Antoine Bosteels at Brouwerij Bosteels Brasserie; Miel Mattheus at Brouwerij De Kluis; Hilde Juressen and Fons Martens at Brouwerij Martens; Claudia De Maeyer at Brouwerij Moortgat; Etienne Detailleur at Brouwerij Riva; Maree Bylett at The Cascade Brewery Co; Antoine Boyer Chammard at Brasserie Nouvelle de Lutèce; Pat Samson and Catherine Van Evans of Carling O'Keefe; Suzanne Howell at Carlsberg Brewery; Harley Madsen at Carlsberg International; Alan Davis of Catamount Brewing; Jose Paz Aguirre of Cervecería Moctezuma; Roman De Wenter of Cold Spring Brewing; Mike Lanzarotta of the Crown City Brewery; James Degnan of Degnan Associates; Jeff Ware of Dock Street; Helene Klein at Dortmunder Actien-Bräuerei; Cindy Wynn at Dribeck Importers; Michael Jaeger of Dubuque Star; Evelyn Wood at EFCO Importers; Enrique Solaesa Rodríguez at El Aguila; Mr Rauschert at Erste Kulmbacher Actiengesellschaft; Jacques Le Grip at Fischer Beverages International; Jeff Davis of Fleishman Hillard; Ferdinand M Schumacher at Frankenmuth Brewery; Thomas Jones of Genesee Brewing; M Sweet at Gibbs Mew; S Nemeth and H Zentgraf at Gilde Bräuerei; Janet ter Ellen at Grolsch Export; Leonie Brennan at Guinness; Brian Miller at Hall & Woodhouse; Nadeen Gonzalez at Hans Holterbosch; Peter Cook at Heaven Hill Distilleries; Annemiek Louwers at Heineken Internationaal Beheer; HV Seidel and St Fischlein at Heylands Bräuerei; Klaus-Henning Ost at Hofbräu München; Gerard Fauchey, A Hanin and Jud Kerkhof at Interbrew; Michelle Grubman at Kirin USA; Suzanne Lanza; J Louwaege at Louwaege Gebroeders; Philip Merrit of Manhattan Brewing; Dider Vallet at Mauritius Breweries; Charles Finkel and Maria Hall at Merchant Du Vin; Steven Forsyth and Jeff Waalkes of Miller Brewing; Charles Cooney, Jr, Curator, Milwaukee County Historical Society; KK Mittu at Mohan Meakin; Hugh Coppen, Harley Deeks and Barbara M Paterno at Molson Breweries USA; Lori Smith of Moosehead; Marc Bishop at Morland & Company; Tom Allen of North Coast Brewing; Dr Herman Regusters at Ngok' Imports; Owen O'Connor at O'Connor O'Sullivan Advertising; John F Phillips at Olde Time Brewers; Joe Shields of the Oldenberg Brewery; Tom Venho at Olvi Oy; Helmut Lindinger, A Seidl and R Gimpl at Österreichische Brau; Doris Haitzer at Ottakringer Bräuerei Harmer; Tapani Ilmanen at Oy Hartwall; Kaarina Linnanen at Oy Mallasjuoma; Barry Lazarus of Pacific Coast Brewing; George Saxon at Phoenix Imports; Lynne Piade; Jaroslav Soucek at Pilsner Urquell; Marita Niedenzu at Privatbräuerei Diebles; K Dürr at Privatbräuerei Gebr Gatzweiler; Mary Thompson of Reinheitsgebot; Amund Ringnes at Ringnes; Gail Rolka; Merja Niomenen at Saate/Tiedotus; Alan Paul of San Francisco Brewing; Arturo R Cuevas at San Miguel; Maiko Ishida at Sapporo Breweries; Eleanor Nakagawa at Sapporo USA; Stacy Saxon of the Saxon Brewery; Greg Schirf of Schirf Brewing; A Prokoph at Schwaben Bräu; Ken at Scottish & Newcastle Importers; C Inglin and M Levrat at Sibra; Paul Camusi and Steve Harrison of Sierra Nevada; Silvia Fadda at Sociedad Anónima Damm; Geraldine Scott at The South African Breweries; Katrin Klein at Spaten-Franziskaner-Bräu; Andreas Hildebrandt at Spaten West; Chris Sherman of the St Petersburg Times; Brother Paul at St Sixtus Abdij; Jana Masínová at Staropramen; Eric Vaughn Smith at Stawski Distributing; Peter Blum of Stroh Brewing; Kiyoshi Morioka and M Takagi at Suntory; Melanie K Webster at The Swan Brewery; Katie Bates of Tied House; J Van Antwerpen at Timmermans; Katie Windon at Tooheys; Jeffrey L Zeisler at The Traditional Beer Importing Company; Mr Aichele at Tucher Bräu; Lilo Eckert of Upper Canada Brewing; Laura Rozza at Van Munching & Co; E Magnani at Vaux Breweries; Peggy Dudinyak of the Vernon Valley Bräuhaus; Vereinigte Kärntner Bräuereien at Villacher Bräuerei; Judy Wicks of the White Dog Cafe; Jim Ford of Widmer Brewing; Bert Grant of Yakima Brewing; Joanne Lazusky of Yuengling; Ryszard Wróblewski at Zaklady Piwowarskie w Warszawie.